THE SHEEP'S IN THE MEADOW ...
HOPEFULLY!

First Edition
published in 2008 by

WOODFIELD PUBLISHING LTD
Bognor Regis ~ West Sussex ~ England ~ PO21 5EL
www.woodfieldpublishing.com

ISBN 1-84683-044-3

Front cover illustration:
Hurstbourne Tarrant 2006.
Shorn sheep in meadow above Ibthorpe.
[Photo: George Purver]

The Sheep's in the Meadow ... Hopefully!

EILEEN SULLIVAN

Woodfield

Woodfield Publishing Ltd

Woodfield House ~ Babsham Lane ~ Bognor Regis ~ West Sussex ~ PO21 5EL
telephone 01243 821234 ~ **e-mail** enquiries@woodfieldpublishing.co.uk

Interesting and informative books on a variety of subjects

For full details of all our published titles, visit our website at
www.woodfieldpublishing.co.uk

~ CONTENTS ~

Introduction

I had to write it. David has had so many people asking him,

"When are you going to write a book?"

I've solved his problem by writing it for him. After meetings whether W.I.'s U3A's, National Trust, Farmer's Meetings or Suppers, everyone said the same, so, here it is. The '.... Hopefully' was added quite late on after I had a struggle to return a recalcitrant ewe to the field!

Eileen Sullivan, May 2008

Hurstbourne Tarrant 2007. The Author with puppy Sid. [Photo: Valerie Partridge]

Acknowledgements

I would like to acknowledge the help given me by Dave, without whom there would be no book. The family have been very supportive and encouraging even when they'd read things I've written about them!

Thanks especially to Peter for helping me with the writing of this book and sorting out the muddles I've got myself into. Also I would like to thank my nephew, Guy, in Australia who drew the cartoons for David's Nuffield report and which we've used since.

I would like to thank The Andover Writer's Workshop for giving me the confidence to write down these stories and which they have had to listen to from time to time. Thanks too must go to Peter Govey, the tutor for his encouragement.

The Author

When we married 46 years ago it was a steep learning curve in every way. Although I had lived in a village, Ash, near Aldershot was a totally different environment to East Brabourne 10 miles from Ashford in Kent. Every time we moved I had to learn new skills and how to adapt to the new situation. Now, at the age of seventy-one, I am still able to be useful, if only in writing a column (mainly about farming) each month in the Hurstbourne Tarrant Parish Magazine. I am much encouraged by the reception this gets. Who knows? I might be tempted to write *The Cow's in the Corn*!

1. In the Beginning...

Chapter 1

"Up you go, boy," said the farmer, Mr. Jack as he hoisted the thirteen year old on to the high metal seat of the horse rake.

"Hold the reins in your left hand and when the rake is full, pull that lever there with your right hand. Try to release it in a line with the previous rake full so that it's easier to pick up."

The field stretched out before David. The wheat had been harvested, the sheaves carried, and now his job was to rake up all the loose bits for the gleaners to finally gather. The song of the skylark and the quietness broken only by the distant hum of the tractor, were all new to the town boy. The hurly burly of life in Aldershot seemed far away. He was so pleased that he had been able to come to Suffolk for a holiday to stay with his father's friend and was already beginning to fall in love with farming. He found it very satisfying to see the rows of straw spread across the field but was ready to stop when Mr. Jack drove into the field. Mr. Jack looked a typical farmer with a tanned complexion and a smiling face. He had five daughters and two sons so was used to boys.

"OK Dave?" queried Mr. Jack.

"Fine thanks, I hope I've done the job properly. I didn't realise that horses produced so much wind!"

Mr. Jack laughed. "You've done a good job Dave. You've a lot to learn about farming but there's plenty of time for that. How would you like to ride Duchess home for me? We'll unhitch her from the rake as it will be needed here tomorrow."

"I've never been on a horse before, Mr. Jack, it would be fun."

"Duchess will be no trouble, let's get her unhitched and you'll find it easier if you sit sideways on the wooden saddle."

With a sack across the hard wooden saddle, holding on to the great collar Duchess wore, David rode the huge Suffolk Punch back to the farm; he slid to the ground and under Mr. Jack's guidance unharnessed the horse.

"Thank you Mr. Jack that was great."

All too soon, the holiday came to an end but by then Dave had made up his mind. He knew without a doubt that farming was the career that he wanted. He had done all sorts of jobs on the farm, from cleaning out the cowsheds to driving a tractor in the harvest field while the men pitched sheaves onto the trailer.

His only contact with animals in Aldershot was rushing out with a bucket and shovel after the occasional horse had passed by. It was grand stuff for the roses and he had customers eager to purchase the contents of his bucket for which he charged sixpence. He wondered what he could do towards his ambition of farming. He asked his father about it.

"What do you want to be a farmer for, Dave? With your education you're receiving at Farnborough Grammar School, you could be a schoolteacher or work in a bank."

"But Dad, I want to be a farmer."

There was no changing David's mind. He spoke to the careers master at school who had to admit that he knew nothing about farming but he promised to find out some details for Dave.

"There's a place near Winchester, Sparsholt Farm Institute, where you can study agriculture for a year and obtain a qualification 'National Certificate in Agriculture' that would seem to be the way forward. You'll have to have School Cert. in six subjects and a years experience before you go."

That sounded ideal to David, and his father approved, although thinking it *would* give David time to change his mind.

Chapter 2

David wanted some animals or something to care for so that he could keep his goal in view. With a small town garden, it was difficult to visualize any sort of farm animal. The problem was solved when a friend of his father's came to preach at the Gospel Hall that the family attended.

"Well David, what do you want to do when you leave school?"

"I've decided that I'd like to be a farmer if possible," replied Dave, "I wish there was something that I could keep in such a small garden".

"I need all the space I can get for my vegetables." interrupted his father.

"Have you thought about keeping chickens? I could send you some day old chicks if you like." asked the visitor.

"Could I Dad?"

His father thought for a moment. "If you are prepared to look after them properly and pay for their food, I'll help you to build a run at the bottom of the garden."

The visitor returned to Suffolk. David managed to find a book in the library about keeping poultry and studied it avidly; he also bought some chick crumbs from the corn chandlers with the money he had saved up. A week or so later, a postcard came for David. "Chicks arriving 5.30p.m on Thursday at Aldershot Railway Station."

David raced home from school on Thursday, changed out of his uniform and pedalled the mile to Aldershot Station on his bike. He waited eagerly on the platform for the train to arrive.

"You waiting for someone boy?" asked a porter.

"Not exactly," replied Dave, "I'm going to be a farmer and my first animals should be on the next train from London."

"Animals! What sort of animals?" The astonished porter visualised being surrounded by cows, pigs, or sheep.

"Well, not really animals, I'm…"

Just then the train pulled in and the porter hurried off. Dave ran to the guard's van.

"Have you got something for me please? My name is David Sullivan."

The guard hunted through a pile of parcels.

"Here it is. It's a bit noisy though. Can you sign here to say that you've received it?"

David hastily scribbled his name on the form that the guard waved at him and took the box, which had air-holes pierced round it from which could be heard a plaintive "cheep, cheep, cheep." On the way out of the station, Dave met the friendly porter.

"Got your animals then boy? Can I see them?"

Dave untied the string that was around the box and lifted the lid slightly. The porter peered through the gap. Two dozen fluffy little yellow balls were all complaining loudly that they were hungry.

Balancing the box precariously on his handlebars, Dave cycled home where his young sisters Maureen and Pat were eagerly awaiting his arrival.

"Can I hold a chick please Dave?" begged Pat as soon as the box was opened.

Dave lifted one of the noisily cheeping birds out and handed it to her.

"Don't squeeze it Pat," he advised.

"I can feel its heart beating," she murmured, stroking its soft, downy feathers.

"What are you going to call them?"

"I'm not going to give them names, silly, I'm only keeping them until Christmas, and then I hope I shall be able to sell them."

"What for?" asked Maureen, looking surprised.

"For Christmas dinners of course. I expect Mum will buy one."

"Dave, how could you be so cruel?" Maureen was really indignant, "I won't eat any."

"Good, all the more for the rest of us," teased David.

His Mother chimed in then, "Where are you going to keep them David? Dad hasn't finished the run yet and I should think they're too small to put outside in any case."

"I thought I'd keep them upstairs in my bedroom. They've got to be kept warm," and he disappeared upstairs with the box.

His bedroom was the smallest of the three bedrooms, scarcely bigger than a box room. He looked around the room and pulled out the bottom drawer of his chest of drawers, his socks and underwear would have to go elsewhere; he stuffed them under his bed. He fetched some newspaper from downstairs to line the drawer and tenderly lifted the chicks into their new home. He then set about adapting his bedside light to hang over the drawer for warmth. He found a dish for the chick crumbs and another one for water and they were soon enjoying their first meal.

The chicks grew rapidly. Dave found their continual "Cheep, cheep, cheeping," rather soporific. He changed their newspaper every day until his father complained.

"Those chicks are a nuisance; I never have a chance to check the answers to my crossword competition!"

Dave then pulled the crossword page out first before putting the rest of the paper in the drawer. After a couple of weeks, the chicks had grown strong enough to manage without the warmth of the light bulb so the lamp was replaced beside the bed. Once they started to become adventurous and hop out of the drawer, his mother put her foot down.

"Those birds must go outside, or else they won't live long enough to become a Christmas dinner."

The chicken run and house were just about finished, so, protesting loudly, the chicks were transferred outside, where they soon settled down and enjoyed scratching around in the dirt.

David was now kept very busy. Before he cycled the seven miles to school each day, he had a paper round, and on Saturdays he helped the local milkman, after which he cleaned out the chickens. He had asked the neighbours to save their potato peelings and any other kitchen scraps, which he boiled up each day after school to mix with poultry meal for the chickens.

He started off by using his mother's gas cooker, but the smell pervaded the whole house so he had to make a fire outside to do his cooking. In addition to all his jobs, there was still homework to fit in with 'O' levels just two years away.

Then a friendly butcher offered him a Saturday job in his shop, making sausages, clearing up, and what David enjoyed most, delivering meat to customers on a trade bike. He had to give up his other Saturday job with the milkman, but there was no shortage of boys waiting to take it on.

As the birds grew bigger and heavier and the months went by, the next problem seemed to be the marketing of them. Some of the neighbours had placed an order with him but he still had about eight to dispose of. The answer came to him one Saturday afternoon at the beginning of December while he was sweeping up the sawdust in the butcher's shop.

"Mr. Wiseman, how much will your cockerels cost this Christmas?" queried a customer.

"Half a crown a pound, Madam, shall I put you down for one?"

"I don't think so, thank you, I'm sure I can get one cheaper than that," she remonstrated and went out of the shop. The butcher turned to serve another customer. Dave dropped his broom and ran after the woman.

"Please Madam, I can sell you a nice bird for two shillings and three pence per pound. I could deliver it to your address ready for the oven."

Dave managed to sell the rest of the chickens in this way, his boss had an idea of what was going on, but as he had no difficulty in selling his own poultry he knew he wouldn't lose by it. He admired Dave's initiative and he was, after all, an excellent worker. David felt rich with the money he had made, so after buying some clothes that he needed, he opened a bank account and saved the rest.

Chapter 3

That summer, he wanted to spend the whole of the holidays on a farm, gaining more experience. His father was still hoping that Dave would change his mind and decide to do something else. However, he spoke to a farmer he knew who sometimes came to take a service at the Gospel Hall where the family worshipped on Sundays and who lived about twenty miles away.

"Arthur, could Dave come to work on the farm during the summer holidays please? He's got this idea of being a farmer, and quite honestly, I'd rather he did something else—like school teaching."

"Of course I can Nat. Will you bring him over when he finishes term? He'll be company for Harold; he gets a bit fed up sometimes with only his sisters for company."

"I'll cycle over with him on the twentieth of July but try and change his mind won't you? Help him to see that it's not all driving around on a tractor and playing about in the hay field."

Years later Mr. Hatt recalled that conversation and recounted how he gave Dave the dirtiest, most unpleasant jobs he could find and wouldn't let him near a tractor. Dave just got on with what he was given to do, didn't grumble and went back to Aldershot at the end of the holiday more convinced than ever that farming was the life for him.

The next year with 'O' levels taken, Dave started applying for a job. He had been accepted at Sparsholt subject to satisfactory examination results so needed a year on a farm to gain practical experience. *The Farmers Weekly* in 1957 had several pages of 'Situations Vacant' so every week Dave scoured the magazine for any suitable jobs. Altogether he applied for forty six jobs and in spite of enclosing stamped addressed envelopes, had no replies except one which arrived the week before he was due to leave school. David opened the letter, noticing the postmark, 'South Molton.'

"Enclosed is your train fare. I may be able to offer you a job if we suit each other. I'll meet you at Molland Junction Station on Wednesday next. There's a train that gets in at eleven thirty a.m."

It was signed by John Ridd.

Dave heaved a sigh of relief, he hadn't got the job yet but at least someone had taken the trouble to reply.

He arrived at Molland Junction on the appointed train. He was the only person to get off at the station which was little more than a halt. He looked around. The only person on the station was a huge man, six foot four at least David thought, who held out a hand as big as a shovel.

"Be'ee Dave Sull'van then?'

"Ye-ye-yes," stammered David hesitantly.

"I've got the van out in yard, c'mon."

Dave followed 'girt' John Ridd out into the station yard where an elderly Bedford van was standing.

"Sorry there's no seat," John Ridd apologised and indicated an orange box for David to sit on. The van chugged its way through winding lanes with high banks, climbing all the time.

"Is it far to the farm?" asked David.

"'bout four miles," was the reply. As David was to discover, John Ridd wasn't a great conversationalist but he certainly knew the road well and managed to avoid most of the pot holes. At last they turned into an even narrower lane and stopped in front of a grey lichen covered farmhouse.

"'Ere we are, boy, t'missus'll have dinner ready for we." and John led the way into the farmhouse kitchen. A rosy-cheeked woman was stirring something in a saucepan on the Aga while a small boy played with some toy cars on the floor.

Mrs Ridd wiped her hands on her apron.

"'Lo, you must be Dave, this 'ere is Johnny," she said touching the child's hair.

"Pleased to meet you Mrs. Ridd."

"Dinner's ready, c'mon Johnny, wash your hands." She picked the boy up and took him over to the sink. She showed Dave where to sit at the large scrubbed table and sat the child in a high chair next to her. She placed a dish containing a big joint of mutton before her husband. David had never seen such a big joint of meat in his life. By way of explanation Mr. Ridd explained, "She were cast last week!"

Mr. Ridd carved slice after slice on to each plate that Mrs. Ridd held out after she had piled them high with roast potatoes, cabbage, peas carrots with a jug of home made mint sauce. Even little Johnny's plate held more than Dave usually ate.

However, Dave had no difficulty in clearing his plate, or disposing of the huge slice of apple pie and creamy custard that followed.

"Now then Dave, us'll go and look at t' farm, I 'spect I've got a spare pair of wellies" John Ridd pushed back his chair. He found an enormous pair of boots for David that threatened to come off at every step. There was a small herd of about a dozen cows in a nearby field plus Molly, who was kept to give milk for the house, in a convenient paddock close by.

"Where do you keep the sheep Mr. Ridd?" queried Dave.

"Ah, they be up on t' moor, us'll have to take the van to see 'em."

They drove about five miles climbing even higher. Stepping out of the van Dave surveyed the panorama spread out before him in stunned silence. The estuary of the river ten miles away glinted and sparkled in the sunlight. The only sound that could be heard was the soft calling of the ewes, the answering bleat of their lambs and the mew of a pair of buzzard hawks somewhere high above them.

David enjoyed his tour of the farm; he hadn't realised such country existed having lived for most of his life in Aldershot. His holidays were mainly spent in Suffolk, where he had lived until he was four years old, had given him the impression that farm land was mainly flat! Exmoor took his breath away with a different view round every corner – and sheep everywhere.It was soon time to return to the farm where Mrs. Ridd was preparing tea, David, in spite of the enormous dinner he had eaten, discovered that he was hungry. Mrs Ridd was making tea using a big brown teapot, having taken the boiling kettle off the Aga.

"Sit 'ee down nex' to Johnny boy," she invited him shyly. He had washed his hands in the outhouse under the continually running pipe, and had left his borrowed boots outside the door. Mr. Ridd came in and sat down opposite Dave.

After pouring out big mugs of tea and a beaker of milk for Johnny, Mrs. Ridd picked up the home made loaf, tucked it under her arm, and carved the first slice, flicking it expertly on to Mr. Ridd's plate. There was no butter on the table, only a dish of jam and a dish of strange white stuff; Dave couldn't decide what it was. Mr. Ridd took a big spoonful spreading it on his bread and topping it with the home made strawberry jam. He then picked up the slice in both hands and sank his teeth into it. By now, Mrs. Ridd had cut another slice of bread and flipped it on to Dave's plate. He decided to follow his host's example; putting a dollop of the white stuff on his bread following with the jam. He knew that his mother would have made him cut his bread in half but she wasn't there! He took a big bite – jam and clotted cream, for that's what it was, oozed out each side and trickled down his chin. He had never tasted anything like it, 'cream' at home came out of a tin labelled 'evaporated milk' and bore no resemblance to this ambrosia. Tea soon came to an end and it was time to catch the train home. The journey to Molland Junction – no longer there, thanks to Mr. Beeching's cuts in the seventies- passed all too quickly. Mr.. Ridd got out of the van and shook Dave's hand.

"When can 'ee start then?"

2. Lorna Doone Country

Chapter 4

It was August. David had been at Eastern Ball for a month now and had lost his town pallor and was looking tanned and fit. He had quickly learnt his way about the farm and enjoyed bringing the cow in to be milked. The first really big job to be done was harvesting, about which Dave knew nothing. A 'pathway' had to be cut around the outside of the field first. Mr. Ridd did this using a 'Father Time' scythe, using long, sweeping strokes, while Dave walked behind, picking up the cut corn and making sheaves, using the stems of the corn to make a band to tie them together. Then he had to drive the tractor that pulled the binder on which Mr. Ridd sat to operate the machinery, which cut and tied the sheaves automatically. It took all day, with a brief stop for lunch, which they had brought with them – great 'doorsteps' of bread, cheese and big home-grown and bottled pickled onions.

As the afternoon went on, other men started arriving and went around the field, picking up the sheaves and 'stooking' them in sixes with the heads upwards. When the field was finished, everyone went back to the farmhouse for a meal of home-cured ham, salad of every sort, jacket potatoes with golden farm butter and lots of crusty bread.

The next day, after all the farm chores were done, Mr. Ridd and David drove to a neighbour's farm and stooked *his* corn and so it continued for a month until everyone's corn was harvested. When the moisture in the sheaves had dried out, they were carted to the farm and made into a rick. There was a rick builder who did all the local ricks; he had to be continually supplied with sheaves, which he used very skilfully. He started off by building a rectangular shaped 'wall' of sheaves and used others to fill up the centre, pushing them down firmly. The roof was made of rushes, which had to be cut from a wet place on the moor.

The weeks passed swiftly. Dave loved the farm in spite of its remoteness and primitive simplicity; it was totally different from the semi-detached urban house where he lived in Aldershot. The farmhouse was made of grey stone and was sheltered from the elements as it nestled into the hillside. It was not really attractive but fitted well into the austere landscape. David's bedroom was above the shippon that adjoined the house and where Molly, the house cow lived. The bedroom was warm and smelled, not unpleasantly, of its downstairs occupant. There were two other bedrooms occupied by young Johnny and Mr. and Mrs. Ridd. Downstairs, there was a dairy/scullery but the large kitchen was the heart of the house where the daily life of the farm went on. There was a big, scrubbed table in the middle of the kitchen, where meals were both prepared and eaten. The cooking was done on the Aga, which had a boiler at one side that had to be kept topped up with water, ensuring a constant supply of hot water. There was no piped water, but the farm could be said to have running water, which ran for twenty four hours a day, through a hole in an outhouse wall and out through the door. As it was fed by a stream it was inadvisable to use it if the cows had walked through it higher up the watercourse on their way to milking.

Bath nights, of necessity, were staggered as there was no bathroom. David's bath night was on Friday so the rest of the household went to bed at nine o'clock and the galvanised 'Bungalow' bath was brought in from its nail in the outhouse. Water was then scooped out of the boiler with a bucket and poured into the bath standing on the home made rag rug in front of the Aga. The boiler contained enough water to fill half the bath and the boiler then had to be refilled straight away. This, of course, necessitated trips to the ever running 'tap' followed by further excursions to top up the bath. At last, when all was ready, Dave fetched his pyjamas and draped them over the Aga rail. He lowered himself gingerly into the steaming water. It was advisable to have the water as hot as was bearable, as it soon cooled down. It was very cosy next to the Aga, with the oil lamp shedding a soft glow around the room. After a long soak it would be time to climb out, there was still work to be done as the bath had to be emptied.

Donning his now warm pyjamas, Dave seized the bucket again. The water was scooped out of the bath and just had to be thrown out of the door into the yard. Having emptied it and wiped it round, it had to be replaced on its nail in the outhouse. On summer evenings it was no bother but when the rain was coming at him horizontally with a howling gale blowing, he couldn't help longing for his bathroom back home with hot water on tap.

Chapter 5

The first Sunday that he had off, Mrs Ridd noticed him polishing his shoes.

"Whe're you going, Dave?"

"I'm going to church, Mrs. Ridd. I like to go when I can."

"There's no church round here boy, it's not the right week for the service at North Molton, they only be once a month. Where'll 'ee go?"

"I'm going to cycle into South Molton as I know there's a Gospel Hall there and it's like the church I go to at Aldershot."

"'Tis eight miles each way Dave, shall I keep your dinner hot for 'ee?"

"I'll spend the day there I think, Mrs. Ridd, and go to the evening service as well."

"What'll 'ee do 'bout dinner then?"

"I can buy something but at home there are often soldiers in at the morning service in Aldershot, and Mum and the other ladies at church, always offer them dinner. I'm sure I'll be all right."

Mrs. Ridd shook her head as she watched him pedal away, fully expecting to see him back at dinner time. She prepared enough dinner for him and set a place at the table for him as usual. Dave eventually returned at nine o'clock just as the Ridds were about to go to bed. His face was glowing with the exertion of the ride home as it had been all uphill.

"You had something to eat?" queried Mrs. Ridd anxiously.

"Yes, thank you. I had dinner with Mr. and Mrs. Cole who lived at a place called 'Bish Mill' and was invited to tea with a chap about my age, Sid Latham and his family."

"Whereabouts was the Gospel Hall then? I can't recall ever seeing it," asked Mr. Ridd.

"It's in South Street set back a bit from the pavement. Everyone was very friendly and there were several boys about my age there."

"Well! I never knew people who'd welcome a complete stranger into their home afore. Time you was in bed Dave."

Chapter 6

Dave enjoyed hand milking Molly the house cow, he loved the satisfaction the job gave as he became more proficient, the 'ping' as the first spurt of milk hit the bottom of the bucket was like music.

He found the rhythm of milking was very conducive to singing and Daisy seemed to appreciate his renderings of 'She'll be coming round the mountain' or 'Onward Christian Soldiers'. He loved the warm smell of the cow, the scent of fresh hay in the manger, and the cow cake that she munched as she was being milked.

She could be rather awkward to milk but if her calf sucked at the same time she would let down her milk without any bother. The calf tended to dribble into the bucket as it eagerly pulled on her teats at one side but Dave learnt to use his leg grip on the bucket to good effect to keep it out of the way. There was always plenty of milk for every day use so Mrs. Ridd made cream, using the skimmed milk to feed the farm cats.

She poured the milk into a large shallow pan which she set on a shelf in the dairy to cool down. The next day the pan was placed to the side of the hot plate on the Aga where it was just warm. As the cream rose to the top of the pan, it was skimmed off when cool with a special slotted spoon to become clotted cream. This was used in place of butter on thick wedges of home made bread during the week. On Sundays they had butter as a treat.

The dozen 'field' cows were kept for rearing calves and after they had calved themselves, Mr. Ridd bought others at market so they had two each.

One evening when David brought Molly into be milked, he noticed that one cow was being singled out by the others and they were trying to ride on her back. After completing the milking and cleaning up he went into the house for his tea.

"Mrs. Ridd, why are the cows trying to ride on Blossom's back?"

""Ah, I expect she's bulling. Jan'll probably want 'ee to take her to his fathers bull."

She put his meal in front of him. "Don't wait for us boy you've prob'ly got a long walk afore 'ee."

Dave tackled the home made steak and kidney pie, wondering what he was in for now. Mr. Ridd confirmed what his wife had said.

"You'll have to drive 'er there Dave and fetch 'er home after t' bull has done his job."

Mr. Ridd senior lived four miles away across the moor. It was a beautiful evening, just right for a walk, Dave thought as he set off at a brisk pace with Blossom in front and a collie at heel. He wasn't able to keep that speed up for long as Blossom had other thoughts; the grass was certainly greener and not only the other side of the fence. Along the banks either side of the lane were all sorts of tasty delicacies not usually available to her. She tried hog weed with its creamy flowers and large leaves, then she spotted the white flowers and ferny leafed cow parsley – or 'Queen Anne's' lace to give its more attractive name.

"Go on Blossom" urged Dave waving a stick.

All went well for a while then Blossom suddenly remembered the calf she had left behind at the farm. It became quite a conflict of wills, but eventually the farm was reached. Mr. Ridd senior came out to meet them.

"You go in t' Missus, Dave, I expect she'll give 'ee a drink. I'll go and introduce Blossom to 'Enry."

"Come in Dave. My, you looks 'ot. How about a drink o' milk and a slice o' the fruit cake I made this morning?"

"That sounds great, Mrs. Ridd," Dave replied and was soon tucking into a huge slice of fruit cake which spoiled him for any other fruit cake he was ever to eat.

As he remarked for years afterwards, "The fruit in that cake was holding hands."

Mr. Ridd came in some time later.

"Job's done boy. Iffen you gets a move on you'll be home afore dark."

The shadows were lengthening as Dave set out on the four-mile walk back. The cow and the boy plodded on for a couple of miles but then as they turned a corner, Blossom broke into a trot. She began to gallop along with Dave running along behind shouting, "Come back Blossom, whoa there!"

Eventually, completely out of breath, he had to let Blossom go, who, free at last, disappeared into the twilight. Dave leaned against the bank while he recovered his breath. He trudged despondently along the lane. Whatever would Mr. Ridd think of him for losing his cow? In his mind he was packing his bags ready to return to Aldershot, they'd never want him now. As he limped wearily into the yard, John Ridd's head appeared at the bedroom window.

"Thanks Dave, cow came home 'bout an quarter of an hour ago, just shut shed door will 'ee.?"

Chapter 7

"Dave, we'm decided to 'ave a couple o' days with my brother over at Minehead. You know enough 'bout the farm to cope for a while. That be all right boy?"

"Yes Mr. Ridd that'll be fine," replied Dave, "just leave a list of jobs for me to do and I'll try and get them done."

"I'll leave 'ee plenty of food Dave," Mrs Ridd told him and was as good as her word. She left enough food in the larder to last a month he reckoned.

They set off in the van for Minehead on the Friday evening planning to return on Sunday evening. David's first job after they left was to milk the cow. He went up the hill to the field in which she was grazing. As she heard the gate open she began ambling over to where Dave stood waiting, her full udder swinging as she walked. As David walked down the lane behind her with the evening sunshine bathing the scene in a warm glow, he could imagine himself as the farmer. He soon had Molly milked and turned out into the 'in bye' field and then went to secure the hen house, there were foxes around so he knew that he must be careful. After eating supper he went to bed early as he wanted to do as many of the jobs on his list as possible and needed an early start.

He let the hens out first and collected the eggs; it was a job he enjoyed as they were still warm. He then brought Molly into the cow shed, released her calf and set about milking her. It was a very satisfying job and he found it relaxing with the quiet noises Molly made as she chewed the cud and the sucking sounds of the calf. He let Molly back into the paddock and put the calf into the orchard before setting the milk to separate. He then put the kettle on to the Aga to make a cup of tea and ate a big bowl of cornflakes followed by toast and marmalade. He found the list that John had left him and worked out the order in which he needed to do the various jobs.

He decided to begin by checking the sheep in the nearby field before riding his bicycle to look at those further away. It was a lovely morning and as the dog gathered the sheep he could see that a couple of them were lame. He managed to catch them and felt like a real shepherd as he inspected their feet and removed the mud that was stuck between their toes. He looked at the list again. Cutting the roadside banks seemed the next job to tackle. Dave hadn't done much of that but he had watched John wielding the brish hook and felt fairly confident. He found the oilstone and used it to get a really keen edge on the blade, he tested it with his thumb, he was sure that he'd be able to cut anything with that. He rolled up his sleeves and set to work, the sun was climbing and it was becoming quite hot. He swished his way along the bank, brish hook in his right hand and stick in his left, he developed a good technique holding the undergrowth with his stick as he cut. If he cut too far then the hook would hit the stick. Suddenly, a careless stroke and the sharp brish hook sliced into his left thumb; startled Dave dropped the stick.

"Ouch!"

Blood was pouring from a cut at the base of his thumb. He sucked it but the blood was coming too fast. He pulled a rather grubby handkerchief from his pocket and wrapped it around his hand; it was soaked through in minutes, he started walking back to the farmhouse while he tried to think what to do. He washed his hand in the stream and found some sticking plaster to put across the cut which stopped the blood a little bit. He was beginning to feel rather queasy so made a cup of tea. He put a couple of spoonfuls of sugar in it although he had stopped taking sugar when he first came to Eastern Ball Farm. There had been no sugar on the table and Dave didn't like to ask for any!

He looked at his hand again, blood was already seeping under the plaster, perhaps Mrs. Bale at the next farm, a mile away, would bandage it properly for him. He wrapped his throbbing hand in a towel and somehow managed to ride his bike to find help. He knocked on the back door of the farmhouse and unceremoniously opened it.

"Mrs. Bale, are you there?"

Mrs. Bale came to the door wiping her hands on a towel" Hello Dave, what be the matter?" she queried as she knew that Mr. and Mrs Ridd were away.

"I've cut my hand, look." replied Dave holding out his hand.

"Sit 'ee down boy," she gasped as he took the towel off. "However did 'ee manage to do that?"

As she took the plaster off, the wound gaped open and began bleeding profusely again. She hastily gave Dave some cottonwool to hold over it.

"That'll need stitching, that's for sure. I'll go and find Charlie, he'll take 'ee to Barnstaple."

She returned a few minutes later, "He's just coming, I'll make a pot of tea afore you goes and I've found an old sheet I can tear up to bandage that 'and." She suited her actions to her words and having bandaged Dave's hand firmly, poured out three mugs of tea. Charlie Bale came in having hastily changed out of his boots and working clothes and they were soon on their way to Barnstaple hospital in Charlie's old banger. At the casualty department Dave was dealt with very efficiently and although his hand continued to throb, once the wound was stitched, he began to feel a lot better.

"I'll just give you a shot of penicillin," said the doctor producing a syringe.

Charlie and Dave were soon back at Eastern Ball farm.

"Sure you'll be O.K.?"

"Yes, don't worry; I'll be fine, thanks a lot for your help. I'll milk the cow and then get myself a bit of tea. 'Bye."

As Dave went indoors, the cat sidled up to him meowing. He put a saucer of milk down for it, it never had any cat food as it caught and ate all the vermin and rabbits that were always around. Dave was beginning to feel a bit light headed and tried to milk the cow but couldn't manage it so Molly's calf had extra rations. He went indoors, his hand by this time was throbbing badly but he managed to push the kettle on to the hot plate of the Aga and found a chicken pie in the larder that would do for his tea. He sat in front of the Aga feeling very sleepy, the bandage on his hand was beginning to feel very tight and he noticed his hand was quite swollen. He compared it with his other hand but discovered that was puffy too. His skin felt tight all over his body. His face felt as if water was being pumped under his skin. He went into his bedroom to look into the mirror there and was appalled. His eyes were like slits and his face looked twice its normal size. Surely a cut on one hand couldn't cause all these strange symptoms? He was very tired and just wanted to go to sleep and was just dozing off when he came to with a start. A car was driving into the yard.

"Whatever's wrong with 'ee?" gasped John Ridd as he came through the door.

"I'm not sure but why are you home today? I thought you weren't coming back until tomorrow."

"My brother weren't well and us felt in t' way but by the look of 'ee, 'tis a good thing that us is home. What's happened to your hand? You be all swollen up too!"

"I cut my hand on the brish hook when I was cutting the bank. Mr Bale , took me into Barnstaple hospital to have it stitched and I had a jab – penicillin I think. I couldn't manage to milk Molly and I haven't shut the chickens up yet."

"Don't 'ee worry 'bout them, Joan'll see to them. I'll take you back to the hospital and see what they've got to say 'bout your hand."

Once again Dave found himself being driven through the now darkening lanes to Barnstaple Casualty Department. The night staff were on duty now and consulted the notes left by the day staff. Dave looked and felt dreadful. His legs were swollen and he had to take off his shoes as his feet were like footballs. A doctor came in answer to the nurse's summons.

"Hm! typical penicillin reaction."

So that's what it was. What a relief even though it meant another injection to counteract the effects of the penicillin. He had been convinced that he had some strange disease.

"I'll contact your doctor as you must never have penicillin again, it could have killed you."

The swelling took a couple of days to go down and Dave had to return to the hospital to have the stitches out but he soon felt really fit again.

Chapter 8

The local Young Farmers Club met at North Molton which was about four miles away from Eastern Ball farm, and they were delighted to have a new member especially when they discovered that he had been goalkeeper for his school football team and was willing to play in theirs. The football matches were rather different from the ones Dave had played at school. There was no beautifully manicured pitch as the cows had to be moved off the field before the game could start. The goalposts were home made, rather rustic in appearance, and it was doubtful if they were regulation width or height. The lines marking out the pitch were, of course, non-existent. The teams against whom they played weren't worried, their facilities were very similar.

"O.K. for Friday night then Dave?" queried the team captain.

"Yes, fine. Who are we playing?"

"Braunton, it's a home game on our field. Seven o'clock kick off."

Dave arrived at the field at ten to seven. The goal posts were being erected so Dave helped by holding the side post while it was banged into the ground with a mallet. The crosspiece was tied on with binder twine and they were ready. The opposing team and their supporters (mainly girl friends), arrived at seven fifteen having lost their way, so the kick off finally took place at seven thirty. It was a hectic game in spite of the heavy hobnailed boots the players were all wearing. It had rained the day before so there were many tumbles and by the end of the game most of the players were plastered in a mixture of mud and cow dung. They washed the worst off in the water trough and wiped their boots on the grass before retiring to celebrate Braunton's victory of three – two at the local pub where, being Somerset, cider was the favourite drink.

It was very bleak in the winter high on the moor and life became more difficult. It was hard first thing in the morning when everything was frozen and the yard was covered with ice. Then it started snowing. Dave had never seen snow like it before. It covered everything and as the farm was situated in a hollow the snow soon drifted. Only the essential work was done and the sheep on the higher ground had already been brought down to the 'in-bye' fields. Mrs. Ridd usually made her own bread and there was always plenty of milk. The vegetables that John grew and had harvested earlier were all stored carefully away.

One day after work, John said, "C'mon Dave, Let's take some spuds to Charlie Bale, He didn't grow as many as we, guess he could do with some."

They went down into the cellar, and found a couple of sacks. John opened up the clamp and shovelled potatoes into the two sacks while Dave held them open. John swung the sack onto his shoulder. Dave tried to do the same but nearly knocked himself out! Eventually they set off across the fields, as the lane was impassable as with the high Devon banks the roadway was full of snow. They struggled across the snow covered fields John leading while Dave followed behind. – He's always maintained that he can never sing 'Good King Wenceslas' with the line 'In his masters steps he trod', without remembering their expedition.

They eventually covered the mile separating the two farms and were welcomed enthusiastically.

"John, how did 'ee know we was nearly out of spuds?" queried Mrs. Bale. "Sit 'ee down by the Aga I'll make a pot of tea for 'ee both"

Dave thankfully lowered his sack on to the floor and straightened up. He felt ten feet tall as the load left him and felt ready for the mug of tea and hunk of fruit cake Mrs. Bale produced.

Chapter 9

When David wasn't needed on the farm, he spent Sunday at South Molton where he worshipped at the little Gospel Hall. He had become good friends with Sid, as well as Don, Alf and Derek who all went to the Gospel Hall too. Derek rode a motor bike and often went out to the farm to collect Dave especially if the weather was bad.

Sid had a suggestion that he put to Dave one Sunday soon after Easter.

"Shall us go across the moor at Whitsun, Dave? There be lots of folk out there who can't get to church and we could take some Bible booklets with us to give them?"

"Sounds a good idea to me, are you going to ask the others?"

"I asked them but they can't manage it," replied Sid, "I thought we could go on our bikes."

Sid operated a simple printing press to produce Scripture portions and tracts, subsequently this expanded into a large business but at that time he had just progressed from a 'John Bull printing outfit to an 'Adana' print machine.

David became quite enthusiastic about the idea.

"I'll get some food together if you can borrow a saucepan from your Mum, Sid. I could get away after milking on the Friday evening. I'm sure Mr. Ridd will let me."

Eventually, a few weeks later, they pedalled off with laden pannier bags away up the hills on to Exmoor. They left on the Saturday morning after all, it was very peaceful, with no traffic to disturb the quietness, and just the bleating of the sheep and birdsong could be heard. Some of the hills were very steep and they had to push their laden bikes, but it was easy freewheeling down the other side.

"Look Sid, there's some cottages down there in that dip."

"Right Dave lets visit them."

With some trepidation they approached the cluster of houses. A spaniel dog started barking furiously as they opened the gate to the first cottage. They walked cautiously past the dog and went round the corner of the house to where they thought the back door would be – nobody ever uses the front door in the country. The back door was opened and in answer to their knock, a woman carrying a young child on her hip appeared.

"What do you want?" she asked.

"We'd like you to accept this," replied Sid proffering one of the booklets. "We know many people on the moor can't get to a church, so we're hoping to give them a portion of God's Word to read about God's love for themselves."

They continued their way across the moor, pushing tracts through letter boxes and chatting to people about God's love when ever the opportunity arose. It was great cycling between the villages in the beautiful countryside and a friendship was forged between the boys that was to last all their lives.

It began to grow dark and they cycled along, looking for another farm where perhaps they could have a corner of a barn in which to sleep. They went round a corner and saw a group of buildings ahead.

"Good evening. We're cycling across the moor, telling people of Gods love for them. Would you like to accept this tract?" Sid asked.

"Thank you, I'll read it later."

"Have you a barn or shed we could sleep in tonight please? We have a Gaz cooker and would be very careful."

"Well boys, you can sleep in the shearing shed if you like, the water tap is over there, just make sure you have your cooker where it won't tip over."

"Thank you very much, sir."

Sid and Dave wheeled their bikes over to the shed and unloaded them.

Dave fetched a saucepan of water as they had no kettle while Sid lit the Gaz cooker. He found the loaf of bread and the marge and rooted around for the mugs and plates.

"Dave, where did you put the mugs?"

"I didn't bring them. I thought you said that *you* would."

"I wonder if the farmer's wife would let us borrow a couple?"

"I don't think we ought to bother them. I know, if we have the baked beans for supper, we could wash the tins out and use those for mugs."

As they only had one saucepan, they poured the water out and emptied the tins of beans into it, heated them up and tipped them into their enamel plates. While they were eating the beans, they boiled the water and then made the tea. They felt pleased with their resourcefulness and decided to get out their sleeping bags.

There was a pile of woolsacks in one corner so they pulled out some of those to use as a mattress and settled down for the night.

"What was that?" Dave sat up and grabbed his torch.

"Go back to sleep Dave there's nothing there."

"I'm sure something ran over my face Sid."

"Help! You're right Dave. Look there's something gleaming over there."

Dave shone his torch around and in the light of the beam they could see several rats in the corners. They banged whatever came to hand which seemed to scare the rats away and eventually they managed to get some sleep.

The next morning after a breakfast of more beans and bread they set off again in the direction of Minehead. They paused at the little villages and hamlets to push a tract through each door and were able to tell some people who were about, what they were doing. They joined the congregation in a tiny Methodist chapel high on the moor on Sunday morning, and then cycled on to Minehead where they treated themselves to fish and chips. They then spent a couple of hours giving out tracts along the sea front, the weather seemed to be changing and the clouds were soon obscuring the sun. They were aiming to get to Lynmouth that evening as Sid had a friend there, and then cycle straight back on Monday to be ready for work on Tuesday. "Good thing we brought our oilskins Sid," said Dave unrolling his cape, "I can't find my sou'wester though, that's a nuisance."

"I hope us can find Mr. Huxtable all right Dave. He lives out Porlock way but I think he'll probably be at the Gospel Hall at Lynmouth this evening."

The rain began in earnest, making cycling difficult and unpleasant as the wind was blowing straight into their faces. Dave was fed up with the rain dripping down the back of his neck, so rummaged around in his rucksack coming up triumphantly with the saucepan. It fitted on his head comfortably.

"Only two miles to Lynmouth now, Dave, us'll just be in time to catch Mr Huxtable coming out o' the Gospel hall."

Dave grunted in reply. The last couple of miles were down Countisbury Hill and the full force of the wind and rain was making cycling very difficult, but, sure enough, as they reached the village, people were just leaving church. They rounded a corner and skidded to a halt outside the Gospel Hall. They looked at each other and laughed. Their faces were splattered with mud, they were soaking wet – and Dave was still wearing the saucepan. Everybody emerging from the little church in their Sunday best looked bemusedly at the apparitions before them.

"Hello Mr. Huxtable, do you remember me?" Sid dropped his bike and darted forward.

"Why of course I do. Sid Latham from South Molton isn't it? Whatever are you doing over this way?"

Sid started to explain.

"Come back into the Hall Sid, I'm getting soaked – bring your friend with you." They all went back into the Hall. Dave hastily removed the saucepan from his head and hoped nobody had noticed it. The boys began to tell the story of their trek across the moor, dripping water on to the floor as they did so.

"Where are you staying tonight boys?" asked a middle aged lady.

"We were hoping that Mr. Huxtable would let us sleep in one of his barns" replied Dave.

"Would you both like to come back with me to Aberlyn? It's a Christian Guest House. You could have a hot meal and a bath and I have some spare rooms."

Dave and Sid looked at each other. "It's very kind of you, but quite honestly we have no money with us."

"I don't want payment. You'd be our guests but I would like you to tell the people who are here on holiday your story."

So it was that the boys spent that night in a comfortable bed after an excellent meal. They were fitted up with dry clothes and their others taken away to be washed. The guests listened with rapt attention and the story of their trek was an inspiration to those that heard it.

The next day Mr. Huxtable arrived with a farm truck to take the boys and their bikes back across the moor. Years later, Dave stayed at Aberlyn as a paying guest and once again had to repeat his story of their trip across the moor.

Dave's time in the West Country finally came to an end as the autumn term at Sparsholt was about to start. His parents hired a car and drove to Exmoor to take him and his accumulated goods back to Aldershot.

"David, if I'd known just what it was like here, I would never have let you come to such an out of the way place," exclaimed his Mother after seeing the running water and primitive plumbing .

3. Learning some lessons

Chapter 10

Dave felt that with the experience that he had had on Exmoor, college would be an anti-climax and with the confidence of youth thought that there was nothing else that he needed to learn. He soon settled down but longed for Mrs. Ridd's cooking. Three chipolatas, a spoonful of baked beans and a handful of chips were no substitute for beef stew thick with home grown vegetables and light fluffy dumplings. Sparsholt was only about twenty miles from Aldershot so when it wasn't his turn to milk the cows or to do other stock duties, he was able to go home for the weekend. He found that the cheapest way to get home was to hitch hike and in 1959 there weren't the problems that there are today. Lorry drivers in particular were pleased to have company and on more than one occasion he was actually asked to drive.

Dave passed his driving test while at Sparsholt. A friend of his father's lived nearby and let him use his Land Rover with which he had become conversant as there was one on the college farm. Dave was quite surprised when he passed the test, as he had been up most of the previous night. The college shepherd wasn't well so Dave had volunteered to do the night lambing. He hadn't really had much experience at driving the Land Rover on the roads either but had swotted up the Highway Code.

Matron was a formidable lady with a starched apron covering her ample bosom. Dave became a particular favourite of hers ever since he singled her out to dance at the annual Christmas ball. She kept an eye on the students, ministering to their cuts and bruises which they sustained mainly on the football, cricket, or rugby fields. Dave played football but elected to act as umpire at cricket as it wasn't a game that he enjoyed much.

One thing he did enjoy was sugar beet singling. The students had to do a certain amount every day but Dave found that the most efficient way of coping with the task was to get up an hour earlier and do a stint before starting practical work or lectures. The course he was pursuing was quite comprehensive covering all aspects of farming but he still preferred the sheep work to any other speciality. There was no fish farming or horticulture at Sparsholt then; that came later when it changed its status from a Farm Institute to an Agricultural College.

During the vacations, David was able to find work on a farm a couple of miles from his home. The first of his holidays was the Christmas break so his chicken plucking experience proved to be very useful. There were several hundred turkeys to be killed and plucked in a very short space of time ready for the seasonal trade. A lot of the casual workers of both sexes shared the same surname, "Luigi," and the family had first arrived in England as Italian prisoners of war. They understood English but were reluctant to speak it and even the children chattered away in their own tongue.

At Easter Dave once more was able to get work on the farm and lined up with the other farm workers to receive his daily instructions from the Farm Foreman who had already made it very plain to everyone what he thought about a College education.

"Joe, you can clear up in the barn."

"Right sir."

"Bill you take some hay to the cattle."

"Yes Boss."

He continued down the line of men.

"Now, college boy, you can take the shandy barrow and sow the sixteen acres with grass seed," he sneered, "Bob, take the seed out to the field and harrow in behind him. Do you understand Boy?"

"Ye-es Sir. Where will I find the shandy barrow?"

"Bob'll show you, won't you Bob?" The foreman laughed mirthlessly.

Bob took David to the barn.

"There you are boy, that's the shandy barrow."

Dave surveyed the contraption that Bob pointed out. Apart from one large iron wheel, there was no resemblance to any barrow he had ever seen. The wheel drove a shaft which operated a brush mechanism that swept the seed out of adjustable apertures situated at intervals along an eight foot narrow wooden box across a framework in front of the handles.

"The field is over there behind the farmhouse. You wheel the barrow over there and I'll bring the seed."

Dave trundled the unwieldy shandy barrow along the lane to the field. It was very hard to get the balance right but he arrived at the place just as Bob turned up in the tractor. The field stretched out into the distance, it would take days to sow. Bob unloaded the bags of grass seed.

"I'll go and get the harrows hitched on, you start there and I'll catch you up."

Dave didn't doubt it. He loaded the box and set off uncertainly. It was hard going as the ground was very uneven and the box tended to tip to one side. He eventually reached the end of the field and laboriously turned the shandy barrow around for the return trip. He could see a faint line of seed at either side of his previous wheel mark. He hoped that he would have enough seed to get back to where the bags of grass seed were, so looked in the box to check, there still seemed quite a lot left. He picked up the handles and moved the barrow to cover the next section of the field. He staggered up and down the field with aching arms and blistered hands for an hour before a tractor drove through the gateway. Bob climbed down from his seat, adjusted the set of harrows that trailed behind the tractor and set off across the field where the seed was scattered. Dave loaded the box once more, spreading out the seed to even it up a bit. The tractor seemed to race along as Dave plodded with the heavy barrow, thinking----

"Excuse me Bob," he disturbed the tractor driver as he had stopped for a quick cigarette.

"What's up boy?"

"Could you lower the front bucket please? Dave explained what he wanted to do and a grin spread over Bob's face---.

By the end of the day the field was completely sown and harrowed in.

The next morning the Farm Foreman worked his way along the waiting line of men.

"Bob, you'd better carry on harrowing that grass seed in behind the college boy."

"I'm sorry sir but I can't."

"What do you mean, you can't?" the foreman spluttered.

"The field is finished."

"It can't be, I'll have a look for myself."

"Well sir, I've never seen a boy move so fast, like greased lightning he was." Bob tried not to laugh at the foreman's discomfiture and the rest of the men knowing the story were struggling to conceal their amusement. Later that day, the foreman drove out to the field; he scratched his head, not understanding how the boy had managed it. Dave and Bob shook hands when they met up later. Bob laughed.

"I thought the old foreman would burst he was so mad he couldn't work out what we'd done. It was a brilliant idea of yours to sit in the bucket and trundle that old shandy barrow afore you."

"Thanks a lot Bob it was handy being able to carry the sacks of seed in the bucket too."

Bob had several pints bought for him that evening as he recounted how the green college boy had outwitted the foreman.

The sixteen months Dave spent at Sparsholt soon passed and David was top student of his year. Once again he began applying for jobs, but this time he had a qualification – NCA with distinction, not a very high qualification now but thought highly of in 1959. Together with the experience he had of sheep made him decide to try and find a job as a shepherd.

4. Milestones and Marriage

Chapter 11

At last. A real job on a big farm doing what he longed to do. He could call himself a shepherd as he had five hundred Scotch halfbred breeding ewes plus fifteen Suffolk rams to care for. The farm was at the foot of the downs at East Brabourne, near Ashford in Kent, which was a very small village with a pub, church and farm. From the top of the downs the sea could be sighted, gleaming blue, ten miles away. Most of the inhabitants worked on one of the farms in the locality. There was a three-bedroom house designated for the shepherd into which we would move when we were married. It was an attractive semi-detached house hung with mellow Kent tiles on the upper half. David was only eighteen, although we were courting we waited two more years before we were married and so continued our long distance courtship by letter. We met infrequently when he came home to Aldershot and I was able to visit him occasionally. Dave had lodgings two miles away from the farm at Brabourne Leas, a bigger village with a couple of grocers shops and a butchers. He stayed with a middle-aged couple who enjoyed the company of young people and whose children had left home. There were three other lodgers and the four boys all got on very well together. It was a busy household. The landlady's husband was a grocer in Ashford and there were various relatives living nearby who visited daily. "Aunt Hilda," the landlady's sister had never married but possessed a great sense of humour. One morning she appeared at the door in great distress holding just the handle of an umbrella.

"Look! My best umbrella and it's gone."

"Where is it Hilda?" enquired Dave's landlady.

"Well, you see, it was like this…" Aunt Hilda always enjoyed telling a story.

"I was on my way home from chapel last night and you know how foggy it was? Well, I had my torch in one hand with my handbag over my arm, and carried my umbrella – although I didn't really need it – over the other arm. As I turned the corner into The Lees, I thought that I could hear footsteps behind me. I stopped walking and listened but couldn't hear anything. I hurried along and the footsteps seemed to get quicker and I was quite frightened. I grabbed my umbrella tightly, turned round and lunged with it – like a sword, you know? Then I hurried on home. I didn't hear the footsteps again but when I went to hang my umbrella up, only the handle was over my arm."

Nobody ever discovered what happened that night and the rest of the umbrella was never found.

Dave cycled the two miles to work each day, taking a packed lunch with him. Although his landlady's husband worked in the grocery trade, the landlady, having the four hungry boys to feed, used rather a repetitive menu. Spam or hard boiled egg sandwiches were usually a feature of their lunch boxes. The evening meal was usually thin home made soup followed by a massive main course, – steak and kidney pie, toad in the hole, fish and chips – with jelly and blancmange or something similar to finish. On Sundays it was always roast beef and Yorkshire pudding plus two or three vegetables followed by apple pie and custard. As a treat on Sundays there was always dripping spread on thick wedges of bread lavishly sprinkled with salt for tea with home-made cake afterwards.

The house was rather rambling with two staircases. The bathroom was huge – apart from the bath and washbasin it contained a big horsehair sofa. Coffee was usually drunk in the bathroom in the mornings as the dining room was only used at meal times. The boys had to sit on newspapers spread on the chairs if they still had their work clothes when they sat down for meals, the 'parlour' was only used on Sunday. One Saturday evening Dave came home from Ashford where he had spent the evening with friends. It had been a tiring ride on his bike as the wind was against him and it had been pouring with rain. He ran a bath and lowered himself wearily into it. Four hours later he woke up shivering in a bath of cold, scummy, water!

On Sunday evenings, the boys often accompanied their landlady and her husband to the little Baptist Chapel in the village. It was always well attended and the services were usually quite lively. On a warm summer evening, Dave had had a rush to get ready owing to a sick ewe that needed attention. The preacher that evening was elderly with a slow, quiet way of speaking. After the service, more than one person asked Dave, "Did you enjoy the speaker this evening, Dave?" or "Good speaker tonight Dave wasn't he?" Dave couldn't remember a thing. When they reached their digs, the boys burst out laughing.

"Why didn't you wake him up Roger?"

"Me? I tried but you know what he was like."

They had sat in the front row as they usually did and Dave dozed off whereupon he acted like a pendulum slumping first on to Roger at one side of him, who gave him a shove which made him go the other way on to the landlady. No wonder the congregation was amused.

Chapter 12

Shearing in Kent was totally different from the leisurely affair that it had been on Exmoor. A week was designated and on the Monday, the sheep from one field, about one hundred and fifty, were gathered into a yard next to the shearing shed. Two shearing machines had been set up, one for Dave and one for the foreman. Bob was detailed to roll the fleeces. It was a warm, sunny day, ideal for shearing as the warmth would make the grease in the wool rise and make the job easier. The first twenty sheep were penned so the shearers could just pull the sheep out one at a time to shear. The method employed was the one used since electric clippers superseded hand held clippers, commonly known as 'left and right' as both hands were used. There had been a report in the Farmers Weekly of a revolutionary new method of shearing practised in New Zealand which involved much wider combs and cutters and was supposed to be much faster. Nobody seemed to know much about it yet, but it sounded interesting.

The shearing went well. The occasional nick to the skin was quickly dealt with by a foul smelling dressing called 'Stockholm Tar', very different to the antiseptic purple aerosol spray that made its appearance some twenty years later. Dave enjoyed the work although it made his back ache and he was glad to straighten up when they stopped for a break. Thirty years later a shearing aid was invented that works in much the same way as a 'Baby Bouncer'. A lamb's wool sling is suspended from a strong metal arm by a spring and the shearers upper body weight is borne by this. He has both arms free and as the metal arm is on a swivel there is complete freedom of movement.

This was a long way into the future and each year Dave had back problems that could only be relieved by lying flat on the floor or by hanging from an overhead beam by his hands. At the end of his first day, Dave had managed to shear fifty sheep and the foreman had shorn seventy five. By the end of the week, Dave had pushed his tally up to about seventy a day and as the weather remained fine the sheep were finished in the week. The fleeces were packed into huge woolsacks, thirty in a sack; these were stitched across the top with baler twine, using an outsize sack needle. They were then stacked in a barn awaiting collection by the wool merchant.

The following Spring a notice appeared in the Farmers Weekly that a Mr. Godfrey Bowen was coming to England from New Zealand, and would be demonstrating the 'Bowen' method of sheep shearing at various venues around the country. He would also teach shearers his method at different locations. Applications were invited for the courses one of which was at Sittingbourne in Kent. Dave sent for a form which arrived about a week later. He filled it in carefully – age, address, job, tally of sheep shorn in a day, signature of employer. The next morning Dave knocked on the office door.

"Please Sir, could you sign this form for me please. It's an application to learn the new method of sheep shearing from Mr. Bowen?"

"I'll certainly sign the form Dave but I've heard that unless you have a tally of one hundred sheep a day, there's no chance of being accepted on the course. There's been such a demand for places that they have to take the best shearers there are."

"Well Sir, if I can get up to that amount will you let me have a week off for the course please?"

The boss thought for a moment, "All right David, the weather will soon be suitable for you to try." He didn't think that the nineteen-year-old would manage it but didn't want to dampen his enthusiasm.

Dave waited impatiently. The next week in the Farmers Weekly there was a report that Mr. Bowen had broken the world sheep shearing record in Wales, by shearing five hundred and fifty eight sheep in a day. So many people turned up to watch that some were perched in the rafters of the barn in which he was shearing.

The weather became warmer and the forecast was good so Dave decided to ask the foreman if he could get the sheep in for an early start the next morning.

"O.K. Dave, but I can't spare anyone to wool tie for you."

As soon as it was light, Dave made his way to the shearing shed and checked that everything was ready. Fifty sheep had been penned in the shed overnight so were dry. He checked his shearing gear, ran the machine while he did the necessary oiling, and pulled the first sheep out. After a couple of hours, he stopped for a break. He had a drink, rubbed himself down with an old towel, and filled the catching pen again. He changed the cutter on his hand piece and adjusted it carefully. It was a pity to break his rhythm after every sheep to roll and tie the fleece but it couldn't be helped.

He gradually became more proficient and by the time he stopped for lunch had shorn thirty five. He ate his sandwiches sitting outside with his back against a wall it was good to get away from the strong smell of sheep. He soon resumed his back breaking job. The flies were a nuisance and it was very hot in the shed with the sun beating down on the tin roof and the heat from the sheep. Gradually, the number of sheep lessened and as he penned the last lot of sheep from outside he knew that he'd reach his goal. He switched off the machine for the last time and as he released the sheep from the yard into the field, he counted them through the gate. "Ninety eight, ninety nine, one hundred."

He knocked on the boss's door on the way home.

"My goodness David have you only just finished work?"

"Yes Sir, I've shorn the hundred sheep so will you sign the form please?"

What was there to say? Dave went on the course, learnt from the greatest shearer in the world, and in the years that followed passed on that knowledge to scores of others. Years later when Dave had the opportunity to visit New Zealand, he stayed with Godfrey Bowen and they recalled the time twenty years previously when as a young man David had learned to shear from the Master.

Lambing in Kent was quite early, at the beginning of March. Hurdles were made of reeds which were cut on the Romney Marsh, eight miles away then pens were constructed from them. These were dotted around the lambing field to act as shelters. The days were short and one particular year the weather was very bad, cold and wet with high winds. One night, the shelters collapsed but the lambs continued to arrive. Their chances of survival were unlikely as the field virtually disappeared under the deluge. Eighteen lambs died that night of exposure, the shock of arriving in such a hostile environment after the warmth of the previous five months was too much for them. In the morning after disposing of the dead bodies, Dave and the foreman surveyed the situation.

"We'll have to move them Dave. The weather forecast is bad for the next week. How about the Dutch barn next to the silage pit?"

"That'll suit me fine Gordon. It'll be an awful job to get them there though."

The whole work force was co-opted to help in the move and soon pens were set up and there were no more losses due to the elements. Bob, one of the tractor drivers did a night shift sometimes to give Dave a few hours sleep.

"Dave, Dave!"

Dave woke with a start. The voice was coming from outside so he opened the window.

"What's up Bob?"

"Dave, you've got to come. I've seen nothing like it. It's horrible."

Dave dressed hastily and ran up the lane after a rapidly disappearing Bob. They arrived at the barn. What is the matter Bob?"

"Look in that end pen. I can't bear to look at it!"

Dave shone his torch into the pen. There, on the straw, still being cleaned off by its mother, was a newborn lamb, alive, but like no other lamb Dave had ever seen before or has seen since. Dave picked it up. It possessed one eye in the middle of its head, no nose but had rudimentary gills like appendages each side of its head. He pulled out his shepherd's knife and cut its throat. Bob was being sick behind the hedge. The ewe had another lamb, which was perfect so she was quite happy.

Alf, an elderly tractor driver was called upon to help Dave one morning.

"What's up then Dave? The foreman sent me to give you a hand."

"Well, Alf, I need you to hold a ewe for me while I stitch it up. She's prolapsed her uterus so I've somehow got to get it back in where it belongs."

They propped the poor ewe upside down against a straw bale with string tied round her back legs which went round Alf's neck. She seemed fairly comfortable but was in a bad way after giving birth to twin lambs some hours earlier.

"Now Alf, hold her nice and steady, I'll just clean as much straw and muck off as I can before I try to push this lot back in. There, that's better."

"Looks all right to me Dave."

"I'll put my hand here and start pushing this uterus back, it came out of here so I hope that I can get it back. There, that seems to be about right. . She's not struggling Alf, I'll just stitch her up – can you pass that catgut to me please?"

"Looks a good job to me Dave, perhaps you should have been a vet."

"Well Alf, seems to me that some things are all in the mind. She hasn't even flinched. We think a needle hurts because we can see it."

" You're right Dave – unless she's dead."

Dave laughed as he took the string from Alf's neck and let the ewe down. – Alf was right!!

A few days later David checked the ewes that had lambed in the night. All was well – or was it. He hurried over to a ewe in a corner by herself. Oh no not again! He wouldn't ask for help this time, it was raining hard and he couldn't move her. Once again he collected all the things he'd need to deal with the problem but fixed her string tied legs behind his own neck. He cleaned her up, and stuffed the uterus back where it belonged. He checked, she was still alive. He made a neat job of stitching her up and when she was up the right way and had had a shot of penicillin went running off to find her babies.

Chapter 13

Dave was employed on other jobs than shepherding when needed. There was a herd of Guernsey cows when Dave started at the farm but it was gradually being sold off. When it was no longer viable to employ a cowman, David took over the milking of the remaining cows. The milking was done in the fields using a Hosier milking bail. This was a milking shed on wheels containing four cubicles with a gathering yard at one side. The cows came into the bail and entered their respective stalls where they were fed an allocated amount of food, known as 'cake'. The milking machine was operated by a stationary engine and the milk collected in ten gallon churns. It was a simple system and suited the farm very well as the cows were moved to various locations on the downs.

David quite enjoyed this work, in spite of getting up at five thirty and cycling the two miles to get there. Unfortunately, his landlady wouldn't trust him to do anything else for his breakfast than boiled eggs, consequently it was years before he could bring himself to eat one again and has never enjoyed them since. The cows were usually waiting to be milked standing patiently beside the bail. One morning four cows had been milked and turned out into the field, Dave opened the gate and the next four ambled in. Three walked into the cubicles but Delilah, an elderly cow suddenly sank to her knees in the doorway.

"Come on Delilah, you can't go to sleep there," Dave urged, trying in vain to get her onto her feet again. She wouldn't budge. He tried offering her some cow cake but she just wasn't interested. The other cows were becoming restless but until Delilah was on her feet he couldn't do anything as she was blocking the way. He tried to remember the lectures he had heard at Sparsholt on dairying. What was that test that showed what cows suffered from? He bent down to the cow again. He sniffed near her mouth, there was a sweetish smell.

"Hypocalcaemia. Of course."

He went to the medicine box in the corner of the bail. Yes, there was the bottle of calcium solution. He'd need a large needle, a piece of tubing and a flutter valve.

He bent down to the cow again and selected a spot behind her shoulder. There, that was the needle in, now the tube; he unscrewed the bottle cap and connected it to the tube. He upended the bottle and watched as the calcium drained from the bottle into the cow. When it was all in, he disconnected the equipment and stood back. Sure enough, after a few minutes, Delilah shook her head, slowly got to her feet, walked into a stall and began eating her breakfast .The foreman called in later.

"Everything O.K. Dave"

"Yes, fine now, just a case of hypocalcaemia but I've dealt with it."

Chapter 14

After David had been in Kent for a couple of years we were married. A tied cottage was available which we could now afford to furnish. I was a complete 'townie' and found it difficult to adjust at first, especially as I didn't drive and we didn't have a car at that time. The bus service was sparse so we cycled everywhere. Ashford was eight miles away but we sometimes rode three miles to the A20 left our bikes under a hedge and caught a bus from there. Groceries were delivered once a week from the General Stores at the larger village of Brabourne Lees two miles away, and there was a small shop in our village for odds and ends. A fish man called every week with very fresh fish caught off the coast at Hythe. Fillets of plaice cost 1/- (5p) each and tasted wonderful. We couldn't afford to go home very often as the fare to Aldershot was over a week's wages. For the first few months friends came to stay with us but when the winter arrived it was quite lonely.

One of the tractor drivers, Alf, lived in the adjoining house with his family. Mrs Shorter was very helpful as my cookery skills were non-existent. She often sent her ten-year old daughter, Shirley, to summon me in for a cup of tea. I'd watch carefully if she was cooking to discover what tips I could pick up. I noticed in particular that when making cakes, she always used granulated sugar; the recipe books all stated castor sugar which was more expensive. I enjoyed making cakes but as Mrs. Shorter's cakes seemed to turn out well, I decided to start using granulated sugar. A week later however, I noticed that she was now using castor sugar.

"Mrs. Shorter, why are you using castor sugar now? You were using granulated."

"Well Eileen, I noticed that you were using castor so thought it must be better!"

I had had nothing to do with animals really apart from cats as we always had one when I was a child so lambing was a totally new experience for me. I didn't like the long hours that Dave was working although I did spend time with him helping with the lambs. We ended up one year with three 'pet' lambs who became very adventurous as they grew older. Dave had built them a pen on the lawn but they soon found ways of escaping and I spent a lot of time trying to catch them. Dave swept the chimney and left the heap of soot at the bottom of the garden. The next day, I opened the back door and in charged three lambs – that had found the pile of soot first! I wasn't very happy as I cleared up the mess, there were sooty footprints everywhere. I had a favourite that I named 'Fred'. He became very tame and followed me everywhere. There was a small grocer's shop in the village which I used if I had run out of anything. I set off for the village shop one day, not realizing that Fred was behind me. I opened the shop door – I couldn't close it because Fred was in the way. The assistant laughed, "Let him come in too." Soon he was the centre of attention as there were some more customers in the shop. He left a puddle on the floor, much to everyone's amusement. He was a good ice breaker as up until then, I had felt very much an 'incomer'.

A farm ten miles away on the Romney Marsh was also owned by the farmer. This is a vast area inland from the Kent/Sussex coast and at one time would have been completely under water. At Dungeness on the coast, the sea is still receding and there are two lighthouses as the first one although originally built on the shore, is now about a quarter of a mile inland. The Marsh is criss-crossed with canals and deep ditches known as dykes that mark the field boundaries instead of hedges and is a very fertile area. The dykes produce thick reeds which were used for thatching hurdles with which to construct sheep pens. The hurdles were rather like miniature wooden five barred gates made by a local tradesman. These were then filled in with the reeds to form a thick barrier. Cutting the reeds on the Marsh was one of Dave's autumn jobs. He spent a few days cutting them with a grass hook (Fagging hook in Kent, Brish hook in Devon). They were then collected by a tractor driver and laid in a barn to dry out.

One evening Dave came home from work looking very sorry for himself.

"Sorry dear, I don't think I can eat anything, I'll just have a cup of tea and go to bed."

An hour later he felt worse than ever.

"Do you think you could go down to the 'phone box and ring the doctor to ask his advice please?"

This was alarming. He hated anything to do with doctors.

As we still had no car and I didn't drive there was no alternative, I'd have to phone the doctor.

"Hmm… sounds as if it might be lockjaw. Has he cut himself recently? He has? That could be it then, especially as you say that he's been working down on the Marsh; it's a bad area for that. Get him to hospital immediately. I'll let them know you're coming."

What now? Another phone call to Dave's ex-landlady.

Yes, her husband would be along straight away. I hastily packed a bag, pyjamas, toothbrush, comb—I hoped I'd remembered everything. We travelled the eight miles to hospital and left Dave in the capable hands of the Night Sister.

"Come and spend the night with us," offered Mrs. Ashman. "We can take you to see Dave tomorrow if you like."

There were some books in the bedroom, including *The New Universal Reference Book*. I took a look at the medical section. Laryngitis… Liver… "Lockjaw – see Tetanus. Symptoms: stiff neck, nausea, headache." The entry finished with the ominous words, "Usually fatal."

I had a bad night and in the morning didn't know whether to phone David's parents before or after he died! Mr. and Mrs. Ashman took me to the hospital in the afternoon where we found Dave sitting up in bed feeling considerably better. Various tests had been done and it turned out to be a false alarm, however, David has had regular injections ever since.

A job that every employee on the farm was engaged in for six weeks each year was pea-vining. The peas were grown on the home farm to precise specifications issued by the firm responsible for marketing. As they became ripe, the peas were inspected frequently to ascertain the exact time to harvest them. The operation would start very early in the morning when a combine harvester type of machine would cut the vines. A green crop trailer drawn by a tractor travelled over the swathes picking up the vines which went into the trailer. The tractor would then be driven the ten miles to the Romney Marsh farm where the pea-viner was situated. The huge machine separated the peas from the vines and podded them, the haulm went for silage to feed the animals and the peas were tipped into big containers before processing.

It was a hazardous journey involving crossing the A20 – before the M20 was constructed. The trailers were wider at the top than the bottom so the tractor had to drive in the middle of the road to avoid overhanging branches. Accidents to telephone and electricity poles were frequent if a driver's attention wandered. Across the A20 the roads became narrower and once on the Marsh there was the added hazard of the dykes each side of the road. Motorists often ended up in the deep ditches especially after a visit to one of the local hostelries.

The trailers had automatic tipping gates which were very sensitive and occasionally were triggered inadvertently when travelling. If the camber of the road was too steep, this too could cause problems as the load was a bit top heavy and could tip sideways with the possibility of a bent or broken drawbar. It was an unpopular job as the urgency of the peas being in prime condition, meant that it was a seven day a week occupation. The local barber did a roaring trade when pea vining was over as it was impossible for anyone to have time off for a haircut.

Dogs then, as now played an important part in the life of a shepherd. Shep was David's first dog and came from a very unlikely source. David's father had noticed the dog in the middle of Aldershot, and although knowing nothing about sheepdogs saw his potential and bought him. He was a brown and tan mongrel with traces of collie showing mainly in the way he held his tail. When he saw the sheep it skimmed the ground in true sheep dog fashion, but at other times it would curl over his back. Shep turned out to be a good all round dog with both sheep and cattle and proved to be a real asset. He loved heights and took every opportunity of jumping on top of anything- including the boss's car. He had no respect for anyone; Mr. Older was most surprised to find a dog landing on his lap when he wound down the car window to speak to David.

Dave lent him to another lodger, Roger, who had to tend some sheep in Norfolk and needed the help of a dog. After moving various flocks around, he stopped at the local pub for a drink leaving Shep sitting in his sports car. When he left the pub, there was no sign of the dog. After calling and whistling the dog, he left for his digs twenty miles away, leaving his address with the publican. In the morning Shep was sitting outside next to the car, soaking wet and exhausted having swum two tidal rivers and covering the twenty miles across completely unknown country.

Fly, a traditional black and white collie, was sent up from Exmoor by train having been in trouble for disturbing the game birds there. After working her for five weeks, Dave was very surprised one morning on going to her kennel to discover that she wasn't alone – she had produced four pups in the night! As she had had no ante-natal care she was in quite a poor condition and when the pups were weaned, had to be put down. Dave sold three of the puppies but kept 'Rosie', who proved to be a really good dog with an unforgettable character. She loved digging for moles – not that she ever caught any but would stand by a mole hill, head cocked to one side and then suddenly pounce and start digging frantically.

As time went on, it became apparent that a second dog would be useful and so Moss joined the family. He was a tri-colour dog, very handsome and keen on his job, too keen sometimes. If he wasn't put into his kennel immediately Dave came home, he would find the nearest flock of sheep and herd them into a corner. The poor beasts couldn't move until Moss was called off. Other shepherds weren't keen on their sheep being moved around. When we left Kent and moved to Sussex, there were no sheep, only pigs so David sold Moss but he had Rosie for years and she proved to be as good with pigs as she was with sheep.

One problem we had with dogs was that as Rosie was a bitch, we sometimes had unwanted callers. The most persistent was a Jack Russell dog which we eventually discovered, lived four miles away. He seemed to know when she had come home after work and we'd hear him barking outside the dog run. Once Dave had found out where he came from, he'd go to the 'phone box down the lane and 'phone the owner who would come and get him. Eventually the owner wouldn't come, "Just kick him up the backside; he'll soon come home then." The dog was very persistent. Dave shut Rosie in the shed and the dog tried tunnelling his way in to her. Dave then sat at the bedroom window with his air rifle and took pot shots at him. After being hit a couple of times he went howling off home but next time Rosie was in season, the Jack Russell returned. Dave had had enough. He then took her into Ashford police station every time the dog showed up. The owner got fed up of travelling into Ashford to collect the dog and locked him up where he belonged.

Chapter 15

After we had been married for about eighteen months, I became pregnant; the baby was due on February 28th, the day that the ewes were supposed to start lambing! Everything progressed satisfactorily until December, when Dave was off work with a metal splinter embedded in his eye. Then the dog needed expensive veterinary treatment and the van which we drove needed a new battery! Christmas was approaching rapidly too!

"Dave, I think you'll have to take me to the doctor. Things are happening that shouldn't be". I had been by myself all day, had a bad headache and had started bleeding. We were soon at the doctors where, after an examination, he decided to get further advice from a gynaecologist who lived nearby. I ended up in Ashford Maternity Ward where I gave birth to a premature stillborn baby. We had reached the hospital just in time as it started snowing – hard!

The following day was Christmas Eve, the snow was thick, and nurses couldn't manage to arrive for work. One lady had to be air lifted to the hospital when she went into labour as she lived in a remote spot on the Romney Marsh. I had been moved from the side ward into the post-natal ward, where things were very busy and I wondered what it was like to hold ones own baby. The babies were kept in a nursery and brought in at intervals for the mothers to feed them. It was quiet in the ward, everyone was dozing and in spite of the fact that it was Christmas Eve visitors weren't expected as the roads were impassable. The doors suddenly opened and in came Dave and a friend, Wellington boots on their feet, faces glowing with the cold.

"Sorry we're late dear, we had to feed the sheep and it's taken us longer to walk here than we thought it would."

We lived eight miles from the hospital!

They were the only visitors that day and in spite of the fact that they had been feeding silage to the sheep and the warmth of the ward released an odour of the farmyard, nobody seemed to mind. The lady in the next bed stated,

"My husband is a cowman so I'm used to it".

I went home after twelve days, the snow stayed around until March.

I was learning to drive, nobody had 'proper' lessons then and Dave used to let me drive the car if we were going anywhere. He was confident enough about my driving to go to sleep, but would suddenly wake up and start complaining about what I was doing. One day when the snow was still around, we set off, I was at the wheel. We had only travelled about half a mile when a car came round a bend. I took avoiding action – into a snow drift! Dave wasn't very happy and stalked off to get a tractor and tow rope. I had thought it was funny, but by the time he returned, I was in tears and he was all smiles.

After working on the farm for another few months, Dave had been there for a total of four years and we felt that the time had come to move on. We had been to a farm near Chichester for a weekend with a group of teenagers from the Gospel hall we attended in Hythe. While there, we learnt that the farmer needed a farm manager for a farm he had bought about ten miles from the main farm. We returned for an official interview later and being offered the job, decided to accept the position.

5. Paternity and pigs

Chapter 16

I discovered that farm moves were totally unlike any other move that I had been involved in. As my parents had 'itchy feet' and moved every two or three years, I felt that I had plenty of experience. I discovered however, that the pantechnicon was a cattle lorry, cleaned out, and the removal men were David and the lorry driver, sent from the new farm. I had managed to pack the china, books and ornaments in cardboard boxes with plenty of newspaper to protect it. The lorry arrived in the late afternoon having delivered a load of cattle to market in the morning. A friend had arrived by train to help us with the move and between us we had everything packed in the lorry by about eight o'clock at night, apart from a mattress, sleeping bags and kettle. The lorry driver set off to cover part of the journey that night. We cleaned the house and said our goodbyes to our neighbours, and then after feeding the two dogs, settled down on the kitchen floor to sleep. We intended leaving at four o'clock so it was a short night. After a quick cup of tea, we loaded our little Ford Thames van. We thought that there wouldn't be much left to take but with the three of us in the two front seats, the mattress in the back with other various bundles, plus two dogs and the cat, we finally left. It was a hair raising journey as the dogs kept losing their footing on top of the load and the cat became very vocal in his discomfort as well as losing complete control of his bladder.

We eventually arrived at Chilgrove just before the lorry, tired and reeking of cats but soon were unloaded and began the job of finding a place for everything. The farmhouse was much larger than our farm cottage and our belongings looked rather lost.

Unfortunately, the electricity hadn't yet been connected in spite of being promised before we moved in. For the next fortnight we managed with oil lamps, candles and a borrowed calor gas stove. What a joy it was when we were able to put a switch down and have light.

Another problem was lack of sewage disposal and no bathroom or toilet. The previous tenants had a tin bath in a draughty outhouse and a privy in the garden. We managed with the privy but had the delight of a bath once a week ten miles away at a friend's house. Building was begun to provide a bathroom indoors. A bricked up room was discovered and excavated to provide a toilet and bathroom. As I was pregnant again, I was very pleased with the new facilities.

The work was very different on this farm as there were no sheep and the farmer had decided to use the farm buildings to rear pigs. There was also a lot of arable land and some rough downland. The previous owners were an elderly couple with a widowed daughter plus young grandson and the farm had become quite run down. It was in a beautiful position on top of a hill, set back from the road with several barns and outbuildings. The view over the beech woods was magnificent, especially in the spring when the young leaves began to appear. One of the first facts David discovered about pigs was that they couldn't be herded like sheep so if they escaped they were very difficult to recapture. Rosie, however, developed her own method of coping with them. She ran along by the side of them and snapped right by their jaws; they would skid to a halt and run back the other way to escape her. One day a group of pigs had escaped while being moved to another building and decided to make a dash for freedom along the road, hotly pursued by Dave and Rosie. Dave was carrying his shepherd's crook which he found useful on these occasions. Rosie performed her usual routine whereupon the animals turned and ran the other way towards Dave. To turn them into the yard he brought his crook into play and caught one of the pigs across its snout. There was the squeal of brakes and a smartly dressed woman leapt out of her car.

"I'm going to report you to the R.S.P.C.A. for cruelty to animals. I saw you hit that poor pig on its nose."

"Madam, if you knew anything about pigs, you would know that the toughest part of a pig is its nose which evolved to assist it to root. Now please go away as I'm very busy."

A very subdued woman climbed into her car without another word.

Chapter 17

Part of the land consisted of very steep banks which were full of weeds and rubbish. These were sprayed to kill off the weeds and after the chemical had taken effect, had to be sown with grass seed. The slope was much too steep to risk with a tractor but David had a find in one of the barns and brought it indoors to show me.

"Whatever is it?"

"I knew of the existence of this gadget but had never seen one. It's a grass fiddle. The seed goes in here and by pulling and pushing this 'bow' it trickles out of here"

Having had it demonstrated I could see how it worked and when David sowed the banks, more than one person stopped in their car to watch.

Life was certainly slower here and although we lived by the side of a main road, it was rather isolated. A farm half a mile along the road had a herd of milking cows where we were able to collect our milk each day.

I passed my driving test in Chichester. We owned a van in which I was taking the test but it developed a fault and the engine cut out every time I slowed down. The examiner decided to abandon the test and told me to 'phone for another appointment and explain the circumstances. I managed to get one for the following week – Friday December 13th! The roads were a bit icy so Dave put a couple of bags of pig feed in the back of the van to make it more stable. The examiner climbed into the van and on looking round noticed the bags of food.

"Those bags won't move when you do an emergency stop, will they?"

"No, my husband was sure they'd stay put."

It was very busy in the city, especially near the Post Office but I managed quite well. "Stop!" the examiner banged the dashboard. I stopped abruptly – and two bags of food hit the back of our seats! In spite of that and also telling the examiner that he hadn't given me a hill start, I passed. I was able to do my own shopping and quite enjoyed the ten mile drive once a week into town and was sent to the local farm suppliers for various things.

Our son Andrew was born prematurely in St. Richards Hospital in Chichester during harvest, weighing just three pounds twelve ounces. The day I came home, having had to leave Andrew behind until he reached the magical weight of five pounds, I found myself standing in a gateway to stop the pigs passing. We had to do a 'Milk Run' to the hospital every day as I was expressing my milk for Andrew. The breast pump had a glass bowl and the inevitable happened one night as Dave took it to the sink to wash. He dropped it on the floor! I spent a very uncomfortable night as a result; Dave rushed the milk into the hospital in the morning and came back with a new pump. Andrew eventually came home still very small, very sicky – Dave was playing with him one day and held him above his head. It was a big mistake! Andrew chose that moment to be sick, right in David's eye! He was quite a miserable baby. I had to hire baby scales from the chemist and test weigh him every time I fed him. He was only supposed to have three ounces of milk but at first he was getting at least four and a half ounces. I found eventually after experimenting that the only way that he could get less rather than more was to give him alternate breasts at each feed! This gave me a very lopsided appearance until he started to grow. When he was five months old, when changing his nappy, I discovered a lump in his groin. Poor Dave came home, as he often did, to find us both in tears but a visit to the doctor confirmed what Dave had thought, that Andrew had an inguinal hernia. I had to take Andrew to see a consultant but as Andrew was still only about twelve pounds, he decided that it would be better to wait until he was bigger.

"Whatever is the matter?"

I had driven all round the farm until I found Dave. I couldn't cope with Andrew's crying any longer. I was worried that by crying so much the hernia would get worse as it was quite large by now. Back to the doctor we went where he was equipped with a rubber truss to keep the hernia in place. I t was difficult to get it adjusted right as the hernia had to be pushed up the canal to where it belonged and then the truss fastened.

Eventually at eight months, he was able to have the operation; I was still feeding him myself at night as it meant that he might be able to return home sooner. He had his operation in the morning and I was told that I could feed him at 9.p.m. Help! Where was he? I finally located him in the sluice room! He had made so much noise that the other children couldn't sleep so they had banished him. I sat by the sister's desk to feed him as it was the only place with any light. The Day book was open on the desk.....

"Andrew Sullivan. Very cross baby!" As he was only dressed in a pyjama jacket and a sodden nappy I couldn't blame him. I was told that I could take him home after the consultant's ward round the next morning.

"Bring him back in six weeks for the consultant to check him. Don't let the dressing on the wound get wet!"

At home he seemed quite sleepy. When he woke up, I fed him. He regurgitated the lot! I 'phoned the hospital,

"Bring him back if you like but there's probably nothing wrong."

I drove the ten miles back to Chichester.

"He looks perfectly all right to me. Give him a drink of blackcurrant juice."

I did, and he brought that back too!

"He must have picked up a bug; you'd better leave him here overnight."

He was fine the next morning although the hernia was obviously not the cause of his continual sickness as he had that until he was walking.

Chapter 18

Having barns adjoining the road made it a very attractive resting place for gentlemen of the road who usually moved off once they saw Dave moving around. One morning David came in to ask if I could manage to supply an extra dinner.

"Who's coming then?"

"There's a chap outside who spent the night in the barn. He's not a tramp but had missed the last bus to Petersfield. He's quite smart with a blazer and college scarf and he has a brief case with him".

"All right then, if you're sure he's O.K."

"Thanks, he'll probably want to use the bathroom too. I've told him there's a bus at one o'clock. He's going to help me stack those bales now."

David went out and I watched with interest as he walked along the path. A young chap stood up from the bale of straw on which he had been sitting. Dave was right; he was tidy but--- why was he wearing jeans with a blazer? As I tidied the kitchen I puzzled over it. I picked up the paper to put it away and a headline caught my eye.

"Prisoner escapes from Ford prison." I read on. Ford was less than twenty miles away. I looked out of the window and could see the man throwing bales to Dave who was stacking them in the barn. There was no way I was going to be able to tell him my suspicions before he came in for dinner. I decided to talk to a friend in Chichester about the problem.

"Elizabeth, what shall I do?"

I explained my dilemma to her.

"I'll ask Peter, he'll know."

"You must 'phone the Police. The prisoner may have been caught and your visitor could be genuine, but it's better to be sure."

I found the telephone number of the police station at Chichester and was put through to the duty sergeant.

"We'll come out right away, exactly where do you live?"

"You can't come yet until I've had a chance to tell my husband, he's asked the chap to dinner."

"Madam, he could be dangerous although he probably isn't the man we're after as he was sighted in the Bognor area."

"My husband was going to put him on the one o'clock bus. It stops at the end of our garden."

"Right. We'll be out then and you needn't be involved at all."

I put the 'phone down took a deep breath and started peeling the potatoes. Dave and John came in at twelve o'clock. It was hard throughout the meal to act as if there was nothing wrong. After dinner Dave showed John to the bathroom, supplying him with a razor and shaving cream and came back into the kitchen.

"Dave, the police are coming out for John at one o'clock."

"Why? What's he done?"

I showed him the newspaper.

"How do you know that's John?"

"I don't but I asked Peter who thought that the police ought to know about him and they felt they should speak to him."

Just then John came back into the room.

"Right John, the bus is due in a few minutes, have you got your briefcase?"

"Thanks for the meal, it was lovely. Goodbye."

Dave came back in a few minutes later.

"The Police car came along and the sergeant offered John a lift into Petersfield. He had no option but to get in but I still think you're wrong."

I was wrong, he wasn't the escaped prisoner. He was wanted by the Police however for breaking into a school- which explained the blazer, scarf and briefcase – which was full of cigarettes which had been stolen from a kiosk. I received a letter from the West Sussex Constabulary a few weeks later, thanking me for my assistance.

As we were a long way from the nearest garage, we always kept a full can of petrol in the barn. This went missing with monotonous regularity until David labelled it "Water" and another can containing water "Petrol," that seemed to sort the problem out.

The following week Dave came in for breakfast, laughing.

"We've had another nocturnal lodger. He was Irish this time with a bike, I sent him on his way and he ran up the road, pushing the bike."

Chapter 19

There was a large herd of deer living in the woods. They were beautiful creatures but created havoc in the crops. A field had been sown with potatoes, but before they started to grow, the deer rooted them all up. David asked his boss, who lived at another farm ten miles away, for advice.

"If you can shoot them, it's all right with me. I'll come and help you butcher them if you like."

Dave phoned one of his friends,

"Winston, you have a rifle I believe."

"What do you want to know for, Dave?"

"I want to do something about the deer that are ruining the crops, would you come and help me one evening please?"

"I'd love to Dave, how about next Monday?"

It was a clear, fine evening, with the sun just setting behind the woods. Winston had a Renault van which had a section of roof at the back which folded back. Roy, another friend was seconded to drive the van.

Dave had managed to borrow another rifle so they set off in the van for the field. As they entered the field, Dave and Winston, an older man of about fifty, stood at the back of the van with their rifles resting on the roof. Yes! There were the deer at the far end of the field. The rifles were cocked ready, the van started moving along the side of the field but the deer were alerted and took off, heading for the safety of the woods. Roy put his foot down. "Bang"! The van hit a rut, the back doors burst open, and Dave found himself flat on his back seeing more than one sort of star. His rifle was pointing skyward. Where was Winston!

Dave sat up quickly and glanced around anxiously.

"Winston, are you all right?" he exclaimed on seeing his friend in a similar position that he had been in himself a moment earlier. There was a spluttering noise and a great roar of laughter spilled from Winston's lips.

"I'm fine Dave, how's yourself?"

They never did shoot any deer that night.

A week or so later, they mounted another hunting expedition when they had more success, shooting a buck which was duly butchered and eaten at a Bible Class supper.

Chapter 20

The next September, David started attending Day Release classes in Farm Management at Sparsholt as he felt it would be helpful to know a bit more about the subject. As he had to work on Saturday afternoons to compensate for the day off that he had during the week, for six months we had no time off except Sundays. However, it was worth it when at the end of the course he received his City and Guilds certificate in Farm Management and also a Full Technological certificate.

We stayed at that job for nearly two years but Dave realised that pigs weren't sheep! He studied the Situations Vacant column in the Farmers Weekly each week but there seemed to be nothing suitable. There was a demand, however, for sheep shearers so he decided to do a season's shearing but it meant moving as we were living in a tied cottage. We heard from a mutual friend that a large house had been purchased in Selsey for partial use as a Gospel Hall. The other part had been converted into two flats and one was still empty, we rented it on a three-month lease and moved in. The flat was upstairs and consisted of a lounge/diner, kitchen, bedroom, bathroom and a child-sized bedroom. A lot of our furniture had to be stored but we felt sure that it would only be for a short time.

6. By the sea at Selsey

Chapter 21

Dave paid a visit to the Bank Manager as he needed equipment for shearing and was able to take out a loan for a hundred pounds! He had answered several advertisements in the Farmers Weekly for shearing and already had a few flocks to start with.

"Careful now, you grab 'old of 'er front legs, I'll take 'er back ones". The old shepherd and his helper carefully upturned the ewe and dunked her in the enamelled bath which stood waiting, full of sheep dip. David stared in amazement. When he had been asked if he minded the sheep being dipped after he had shorn them, he hadn't visualised anything quite like that. Neither had he imagined using a beautiful crimson Axminster carpet to shear on! He had asked if there was a board or something on which he could shear as he needed a clean surface as the wool would be downgraded if any mud or straw was mixed in.

"We've just the thing. We cleared out an 'ouse yesterday, that's where we fetched the bath from, 'ere will this do?" The shepherd produced the lovely carpet, far better than anything we had at home. "It's far too good to shear on. Haven't you anything older?"

"No, if that'll do you, go ahead and use it."

The bath plug was operational and the water was run in via a hose pipe. The ewes didn't seem to mind and shook themselves vigorously when they were released. The shepherd and his assistant had garbed themselves in oilskin trousers and coats and exchanged their leather boots for wellies so were ready for anything.

It was a lengthy business but Dave just pushed the sheep into a holding pen as they were shorn and they were removed from there and given their bath.

Another farm he went to had eleven hundred sheep to be shorn, so Dave knew everything must be as easy and efficient as possible if he was going to get them shorn in the ten days he had allowed for them. There was a motley assortment of tumbledown sheds and barns surrounded by a sea of dry churned up mud, not the most salubrious of places.

"Tom, can I see where to put the trailer please?"

"I thought we could use the 'ere shed and rig up a catching pen just 'ere," volunteered Tom, indicating with his hand where he meant.

"That's fine Tom, where's the nearest electrical socket to plug the machine into?"

"I ain't got any 'lectric out 'ere boy. Haven't you got a generator? Shearers last year 'ad their own."

"Well Tom, unless you can borrow one, I won't be able to do your sheep. Give me a ring when you've sorted it out."

Twenty years later a shearing machine was invented that would run from a 12 volt Land Rover battery which revolutionised shearing but that was in the future.

A couple of weeks later, the 'phone rang.

"I've got the 'lectric connected now Dave when can you come?" Tom sounded eager to get started,

"I'm free next Monday so I'll make a start then."

"Don't bring any grub with you, I'll see to that and you can eat along o' me".

When Dave arrived at seven o'clock the next Monday as arranged, Tom came out of the farmhouse to meet him. His resemblance to 'Steptoe' was uncanny. The same hooked nose, designer stubble, gaberdine mac tied around the middle with binder twine, greasy cap plus wellies.

"I got the 'lectric fixed, no bother, come and see." Tom said eagerly. Dave followed him to the barn where, on the wall was a brand new socket with the meter above reading zero.

Dave set up his machine while Tom gathered the first two hundred sheep into the pen. They appeared to have a heavy coat and were looking good. However, once their fleece was removed, they were quite poor, very scraggy with protruding bones resembling hat racks. This made them difficult to shear and a couple of them were in such poor condition that they died on the board while they were being shorn.

When Tom straightened up and announced that it was dinnertime, Dave was only too pleased to switch the machine off and follow Tom into the house. He lived alone as his wife had left him some years before. Dave washed his hands at the kitchen sink and sat down at the table after pushing the cat off the chair. From the larder, Tom fetched the biggest ham that Dave had seen plus a loaf of crusty bread, some butter and a big jar of pickles. He cleared a space for the food amongst the piles of old newspapers and what looked like bills and hunted in a drawer for a carving knife. He took it to the door and proceeded to sharpen it on the, not very clean, doorstep.

"Right Dave, are you hungry?" Tom started carving slices of the ham, holding it steady with his other hand which was green from handling the greasy fleeces and pulling the daggings off the britch end of the fleece. Tom piled several slices on to the plates and pushed one across to David.

"There, help yourself to bread and pickle, I reckon that'll keep you going. I'll just put the kettle on."

The teapot which was standing by the side of the filthy gas stove was black with age, but the tea was hot and strong which was what Dave needed. The ham was excellent and the simple meal was enough to set them up for the afternoons shearing.

A few hours later, Tom summoned him in for tea; Dave wondered what would be on the menu this time. Tom had 'laid' the table – with ham, bread, butter, and pickle. There was still an awful lot of ham left even after the very generous helpings Tom had served up, perhaps he had it for breakfast as well, Dave thought. By the end of the week Dave felt that he never wanted another slice of ham and as Tom didn't have a 'fridge it was beginning to taste rather odd. There was an occasional difference sometimes they had tomatoes instead of pickle!

A couple of days later, shearing was well under way when a vehicle came into the yard. "Shan't be a minute, Dave," said Tom as he scurried away.

He came back five minutes later.

"Well, what do you think of this Dave?" asked Tom proudly as he strutted before Dave in a brown gaberdine mac.

"That's very nice Tom, fits you a treat."

"Got it off the dustman," ventured Tom, "he knows what I like and saves anything that he thinks might fit me."

Tom incidentally was one of the richest men in Sussex as the quarrying rights had been sold for the gravel that was beneath his farm. As it was not yet needed, Tom was able to continue farming there.

Dave went home on the Saturday evening. There were still a couple of days shearing left but Dave had arranged to provide his own meals as Tom was going away. Dave walked in the door. "I'm home dear," he called. I had his meal all ready, "Come and sit down Dave, I've got your favourite, salad and ham!"

Another young couple lived in the downstairs flat and we became firm friends especially as they had a young baby too.

The two little boys spent a lot of time together; but they were put for their rest at opposite ends of the garden in their prams. Terence was a placid child who just ate, slept and played. Andrew was the complete opposite, very restless, still sick most of the time and a poor sleeper. The flat was about ten minutes walk from the beach and lifeboat station so whenever we heard the maroon go off, we'd bundle the babies into their prams and rush off to see the launch. Selsey lifeboat is launched down a ramp and enters the water very dramatically with a splash so it was always a thrill to watch.

Chapter 22

Dave still scanned the Farmers Weekly each week for a job and soon a suitable one was advertised.

"Farm Manager required good with sheep. North Hampshire. Arable and sheep. 500acres. Able to start in June if possible."

Dave had shearing bookings until the middle of July, it could be a problem. He sent off his details (no C.V. in those days) and soon had a reply asking him to attend for an interview. I was invited as well so a friend offered to have Andrew. The interview was timed for 10.a.m. so we had to leave quite early to deliver Andrew first. As we descended Hurstbourne Hill for the first time we saw the valley beneath us and hoped this might become our home. As we travelled through the village with its abundance of thatched cottages we began to realise what a special place it was.

The interview with Dave's prospective employers was quite satisfactory although David learnt that he was the youngest applicant. He was still only twenty-four but his experience and love of his work, especially the sheep, proved to be the deciding factor and the job was his.

He was asked one rather odd question during the interview,

"What religion are you? We know it's an unusual question to be asked but we need a man with principles."

Dave explained what he believed and also that apart from essential stock work he didn't agree with working on a Sunday.

"The men won't like that, as at harvest time they work seven days a week and would miss the overtime money."

"They'd work until 10p.m. six days each week so would actually receive more money. The other benefit is that the combine would only have to be prepared for six days so it would save time."

When Dave was given the job, it was decided that his system would be tried to see if it worked.

7. "Hurstbourne Tarrant? Where's that?"

Chapter 23

The late starting was no problem so a month later we moved to Hurstbourne Tarrant and have lived there ever since. David has worked for two employers and has also been self-employed with his own flock of sheep for twenty years.

The first morning we were in our new house, there was a knock at the back door. A man stood there, his face beaming.

"Hallo brother, we prayed you in!"

Gordon was from the local Gospel Hall and when the congregation there heard that we had applied for the job and would be joining them; they made it a matter of prayer. The Gospel Hall was at a village four miles away and we were pleased to discover another young couple there with a little girl a few months older than Andrew. Nigel was a farmer about ten miles from us over the Wiltshire border. His wife, Marion, was from New Zealand and eventually they returned there. We became good friends and still keep in touch forty years later.

We lived in a four bedroomed house, one of a row, or rank, of five, ours had been two cottages but had been made into one. The farm gardener and his wife lived in the next house, an older couple but very willing to care for Andrew if the need arose. An elderly lady lived the other side of us, one house was used by a 'weekender' and the other rented out to a young couple with two little girls.

Rosie, the sheepdog moved with us and we bought another puppy, Brock; he had a white badger like blaze down his nose and looked a typical collie.

We quickly settled down and the farm work, although very different from the shepherding that David did in Kent, was very challenging. As we arrived in July, the first major job was harvesting the four hundred acres of corn. This necessitated altering the existing system of working until seven o'clock each evening for seven days each week, and changing to a six day week and finishing at ten o'clock. As Dave had predicted, this meant there was more overtime worked rather than less with the added advantage that the tractors only had to be prepared six days instead of seven. Later when the tractor drivers were married and had children, they appreciated having Sunday off to spend with their families.

Peter was born eighteen months after we moved to Hurstbourne, he arrived just a fortnight early weighing six pounds and was a breech delivery! It used to be quite a problem in the mornings as at one time I had twelve baby lambs to bottle feed in the garden as the ewes hadn't been culled properly the previous year and many of the ewes had 'blind' udders. Peter needed feeding and Andrew wanted his breakfast as well as Dave coming home at nine o'clock for his breakfast.

Peter, as Andrew had been, was a very 'sicky' child. Even when he was crawling, I still had to follow him round to mop up. One day as I went to clear up a puddle, something moved in it. I thought at first that it was a potato shoot. I gingerly pulled it out and discovered that there were three objects, each about two inches long. My first thought was to flush them away but as Dave was expected home I decided to show him. His reaction was to put them in an envelope and take them to our doctor who lived in the village and whom we knew very well.

He was most interested – in spite of the fact that he was in the middle of a dinner party at the time – and sent the worms to a professor at The Hospital for Tropical Diseases in London. They were identified as being Toxacara Cattis and it was most unusual for them to grow to the adult form in a human and could cause blindness or lung problems. The boys had to have blood tests and skin tests and although they were very healthy children on the whole it was decided to admit the boys to hospital for further tests and treatment at The Hospital for Tropical Diseases near St Pancras Station in London. The consultant was based there and Toxacara fitted into no particular medical category. I was able to stay with the boys and we had our own room but with no facilities for caring for a baby of fifteen months and a toddler of three years old. I had to wash nappies out by hand in the wash basin and dry them on the radiator, – no disposables in those days. Meals were a problem too as only adult meals were supplied at awkward times of day that didn't always coincide with the routine that I tried to maintain with the boys. They were both rather traumatised, more so by the further tests they had to have. I was given a medicine glass of liquid for each of them and told that they had to drink it. Andrew co-operated and swallowed it with a reward of a sweet but there was no way that Peter was going to drink it. I took him to the staff-nurse. "He won't drink it".

She took him from me, "Give me the glass and go away." Five minutes later she returned him to me, "All gone," she smiled. I cuddled my children but never did discover what was in the glass. The experience had a lasting effect on Pete though and he would never take any medicine although he would swallow tablets.

Peter developed a cough so had to have a chest X-ray but again, no facilities for children. I had to don a heavy rubber apron and hold him down on the table while they X-rayed him with Andrew sobbing in the background. There were some good things however. My father-in-law worked in London and visited as often as he could, he was a civil servant and would flourish his briefcase with its official badge and was admitted without question. Occasionally, he'd be able to take us out and we visited various London parks which did help a lot. One memorable Saturday, Dave obtained permission to take us to The Regents Park Zoo which was within walking distance. I had borrowed a twin push chair from a friend for our visit to London which was a real help. After a fortnight we were allowed home with various pills to give the boys but had to travel to London every month for blood tests and an examination. This lasted for six months until eventually, we were told that we needn't go any more and apart from a scare with Andrew's eyes when he was eight years old which could have been caused by Toxocara, the boys never had any more trouble.

Our doctor wrote an article for the British Medical Journal which was published – complete with photographs of Peter's worms!

As the boys grew up they were very good company for each other and the house always seemed full of their friends. Dave's father had made a 'rope' ladder that could be carried around and tied up in a tree. Andrew and two of his friends went off into a nearby copse one afternoon in the summer holidays.

He came walking into the house by himself.

"Where's the others?"

"Well, Greg went home and I think that Paul has broken his arm!"

"Whatever do you mean? Where is he?"

"He fell off the ladder and is still up in the wood."

I 'phoned his mother. There was no reply.

"He says that his Mum's gone shopping."

We went up the hill to the copse. Paul was sitting on the ground cradling one arm with his other hand. It was obvious that there was something wrong. I helped him down the hill and saw another neighbour.

"Phyllis, could you come to the hospital with me please. We think that Paul has broken his arm."

Phyllis made arrangements for her children and we drove to the hospital. Paul's arm *was* broken so it was set and plastered. We drove home his mother had returned and was very philosophical about it. It mended perfectly in the end and we threw away the rope ladder!

When the boys were a bit older they bought a little tent and slept out in the garden. They soon outgrew that and wanted to go further afield. Philip, a friend of Andrew's also had a tent so they were able to camp in a field belonging to a friend. Peter and Simon, Philip's brother and Peter's best friend had to wait until they were a bit older. They bought themselves a 'Gaz' stove and became quite adept at heating up soup or baked beans!

The seasonal stream ran through some of the fields. One in particular was adjacent to the barns were David sometimes did his shearing. We had taken Dave's tea to him one day and the boys were playing 'Pooh sticks' but they soon tired of that.

"Dad, Can we use this as a canoe please?"

'This' was the footrot bath that Dave used for the sheep! It made a splendid canoe and once they located some wood suitable for paddles were blissfully happy. The water wasn't very deep but they cleared away some of the water weed and soon had a good stretch of water.

Dave had a bunch of sheep to get across the stream. Among them was a blind ram, who was good at his job even if he couldn't see where the ewes were. The sheep that day were being very awkward and refused to get their feet wet. In sheer desperation, Dave grabbed hold of the blind ram and walked backwards into the water with him. Suddenly, the ram got the idea, pushed Dave into the water and used him as a bridge so the others followed suit. Dave declares that some of them never got their feet wet! Dave's employer had a new bungalow built for us which was very comfortable and convenient, but it was quite near to the grain dryer and consequently rather noisy and dusty during harvest. As the men worked long hours during harvest, the combine drivers' wife, Margaret, and I would take a picnic tea to the men in the harvest field with our children. This gave the Dads an opportunity to see them which otherwise would have been denied them as the men started early in the morning and finished late at night. It also gave us the chance to sort out any problems that may have arisen, and, later in the season to pick the blackberries that were usually plentiful around the fields. The sheep rather had to take second place during this time but there wasn't much to do until October when the ewes were checked thoroughly for any problems and new rams bought ready for tupping in November.

Chapter 24

Rams were usually bought at Wilton Sheep Fair which is held four times each year at monthly intervals commencing in August. Dave usually went to the September and October fairs, sometimes taking sheep to sell, or else to buy rams. The Fairs were held in the same field every year so the ground was very uneven where the rows of pens stood. It was incredible to me that the site had changed so little over the years. The sheep were transported there by lorry whereas at one time they would have walked. The field was surrounded by houses and it seems only a matter of time before Wilton Sheep Fair has to succumb to 'progress'. The atmosphere was unique with buyers and sellers from a very wide area from Sussex to Devon. On a fine Autumn morning it was a magical place to be with the smell of sheep pervading everywhere. The ewes and shearlings were usually penned in groups of twenty to fifty, the shepherds tried to grade them so the sheep in any one pen would match up with each other. Rams were penned and sold singly and the best ones fetched several hundred pounds.

The boys and I loved to join Dave there although he usually left in the morning much earlier than we did. We'd get a catalogue and look for the pen numbers where his sheep were. He'd be leaning on the fence extolling the good points of the pen to whoever wanted to know. Selling began at ten o'clock when the auctioneer's assistant walked round ringing a big brass bell. The auctioneer climbed into his booth while everyone either stood by the ring or sat on bales of straw piled high on a trailer to form tiered seats. The roustabouts drove the first lot into the ring. They would be kept busy all day just moving sheep around. They were casual labourers employed by the auctioneers but most of them would know something about sheep.

"Right! Who'll start me off? A fine pen of two-tooths gentlemen. Must be worth forty pounds each. Forty anywhere? Thirty? Right, at the back. Twenty five." Once more the age old job of selling sheep had begun. Some pens were worth more than others although to the untrained eye they looked no different than any other. Some sellers had made a name for themselves with well-bred sheep or were particularly skilful in presenting them. The pens of sheep were brought along alleyways to the ring and returned by a different route so there was a continual supply of sheep. After purchasing what sheep were wanted, the buyer would go to the 'office' marquee to pay for them, and then find a haulier to transport them back to the farm. Our local haulier was a very flamboyant character with a matching red and white spotted tie and handkerchief .He stood in a prominent place where his customers could find him easily.

One year Dave bought a lovely Suffolk ram. They're the ones with black faces and have a deep bass 'Baa'. That particular day he hadn't intended buying anything so we had gone in the car.

"How are you going to get it home Dave?"

"I don't think it's worth getting it taken home by lorry, we'll put it in the back of the car". We had an estate car at the time and the boys weren't with us so the beast was duly loaded up and stood in the back quite happily with his head between us. The only trouble was that it must have been eating cabbages and we had to travel with the window down all the way home!

It was a good meeting place too for meeting acquaintances. Tom from our Chichester days usually attended complete with cap and gaberdine mac. Later, Dave taught part time at Sparsholt Agricultural College and his students would gather at Wilton and compare experiences. In 2001 of course there were no markets or sheep fairs owing to the Foot and Mouth crisis, so shepherds and farmers felt more isolated than ever as they couldn't meet up to talk over the problem.

Chapter 25

We usually kept two sheep dogs that were very essential to Dave's job, especially as the sheep changed fields by walking along the road. Dave tried to move them early on Sunday mornings when there wasn't much traffic. As most times they had to walk along a main road, it could be quite tricky. Our main dog was called 'Briar', -prickly by name and nature. He was quite a nervous dog and the local postman had a complete antipathy to him. He had tried to make friends with the dog but Briar mistook his intentions one day when Henry approached waggling his hand at him and bit him. From then on Henry carried a stick, and kept a wide berth.

One day, Dave was moving a flock of about a hundred sheep along the road when he saw a figure on a bike approaching.

"Is that dog around?" called Henry.

"Yes, he's bringing the sheep at the back."

"Is he under control?"

"Well, he's working so shouldn't bother you".

Henry stood with his back against a wall and arranged his bike in front of him like a fence. Dave strode by followed by the flock of sheep with Briar and Brock behaving very professionally at the rear, weaving from side to side, keeping the sheep moving. The cavalcade passed uneventfully and Henry began extricating himself from his self built compound. Suddenly there was a yell! Henry was in the process of mounting his bicycle when a black and white beast turned from his duties and helped Henry on his way!

Briar was a most attractive dog, a typical collie with a magnificent tail complete with traditional white tip on the end. He had a 'girl friend' living a quarter of a mile away, 'Flanders', whom his owner declared was really in love with Briar.

One night we couldn't find Briar anywhere so reluctantly went to bed leaving him out.

The next morning he was outside the door looking very sorry for himself with blood coming from his mouth. At first Dave couldn't see what was wrong, but on examining him, discovered that somehow he had lost part of his tongue. He drank copiously but slurped up the water and we fed him some porridge, and as he didn't seem too bad, we assumed that he had had a car accident,--That was until he disappeared again! Dave found him at his girl friend's house then everything fell into place. He had tried to find a way in to his beloved and discovered the low-level letterbox. Unfortunately, his head wouldn't go through but his nose did. He panted in delight but on withdrawing his face, didn't know that the letterbox was spring loaded! The owner had heard a commotion early in the morning but still didn't realise what it was – even when she found what looked like a piece of meat on the door mat!

He had another catastrophe a few years later at the other end of his body. Whilst riding on the footplate of a rather elderly open tractor one day, there was a sudden agonised yelp from Briar. Dave stopped the tractor and discovered that the dog's tail had become entangled round the exposed brake drum. There was no way that he'd be able to release it without help as the tractor would have to be reversed and the tail unwound. Briar was becoming frantic as he tried in vain to free himself.

"Lay down boy," soothed Dave, patting the dog on the head and speaking calmly to him. Gradually his cries of distress quietened and he sat, tail firmly held by the brake drum while Dave ran for help. A tractor driver wasn't too far away and he slowly reversed the tractor as Dave eased the tail free. It looked in a bit of a mess, rather flattened, obviously broken and Briar seemed in a lot of pain. Dave quickly drove him into the vet five miles away and after careful examination the vet made the decision to amputate the tail the next day. He didn't take all of it off, but it left Briar a very embarrassed dog, especially when the bandage was first removed and the stump revealed. He'd sit on it so that it couldn't be seen as of course the white tip of his magnificent plume like tail had gone.

A third thing happened to mar his handsomeness. He loved riding through the village on the flat trailer as he could see all the other poor dogs that had to walk. Passing one animal being walked at the end of a lead, he began barking furiously. He ran from one end of the trailer to the other but caught his jaw on the back of the trailer. The barking stopped abruptly and when Dave investigated, discovered Briar's jaw hanging uselessly. Taking the dog to the vet had been a traumatic event ever since he had lost half his tail. After all what else might the vet cut off? This time he was in too much shock to give him the sedative that the vet had given Dave to administer before each surgery visit and once again he had to visit the vet in a hurry. The vet wired the jaw at each end to keep it in place so it was back to porridge again for a few days. It should have been longer but somehow, Briar managed to remove the wire! The jaw had partially knitted together but ever after Briar would sometimes develop a lopsided leer but in spite of everything the local bitches still found him very attractive.

He was, however, an excellent sheep dog, probably the best that Dave ever owned. He could anticipate commands, even to the extent of running along garden walls to reach a vulnerable gap when moving sheep along the road.

Chapter 26

Sheep keeping was not without its hazards. The boys loved helping to move the sheep and became quite a help, but one day they returned from a job scratching themselves

"A sheep ran the wrong way so we tried a rugby tackle on it," explained Andrew

The sheep were on their way to be dipped but I could scarcely carry out the same treatment on the boys so they had to make do with a Dettol bath.

The boys enjoyed their school days at the village school which was reached by crossing a wooden footbridge across the stream. This was a 'winterbourne' usually rising in November or December and flowing until June or July. The schoolchildren would lean over the playground wall and 'fish', Pooh Sticks could be played on the way to or from school. The recreation ground adjoining the school was used in the summer for games and at playtimes and also of course for school sports.

Andrew asked if he could keep a goat which seemed a reasonable request as the village green was the other side of our garden fence. Dave asked around and a neighbouring farmer had a young nanny kid which duly joined the family. She was black and white; Andrew named her 'Susie'. Dave created a sleeping place for her in the shed with a raised platform as goats like being up from the floor. Every morning before Andrew went to school he attached a chain to her collar and led her out on to the green carrying with him a sledge hammer. Dave had made a long metal stake at the local blacksmiths which Andrew banged into a fresh area each morning to which was fastened Susie's chain. He'd bring her back into the shed before it became dark, groom her, and give her oats to eat.

Occasionally, I'd either have a 'phone call or somebody would call with the message.

"The goat is loose."

I'd have to leave everything I was doing, grab a piece of bread and rush out to entice Susie over so that I could secure her again! It made me feel like Janet in 'David Copperfield' answering to the cry of his Aunt, Miss Betsy Trotwood,

"Janet! Donkeys!"

After having Susie in the family for about a year, Dave thought that if she had a kid and produced milk, we could use it for any lambs that needed it as it is very similar to ewe's milk. He took her to a friend's billy goat and she had two kids, one of each sex. After they were weaned we were able to sell them and Dave had the job of milking Susie twice a day. The boys and Dave used the milk but I didn't like the taste so the milkman still called three times a week for my benefit.

Chapter 27

"Look Dave, there's going to be a party on the Playing Fields to celebrate the Queen's Silver Jubilee." It looked as if it would be fun for the children with a fancy dress parade through the village for anyone that wanted to take part.

We decided to try and enter but didn't know quite what to dress in. Margaret, the tractor driver's wife and her children were going to join in too.

Dave came in one evening with a grin on his face,

"Look at these fertilizer sacks. We could make tunics and hats from them."

The sacks had Union Jacks on both sides. I could see what he meant so we set to work....

The big day arrived, it was overcast but dry. We had to assemble at Ponting's (the hauliers) yard at two o'clock. 'We' being, our family of four plus Margaret's family of four (her husband, Rodney was organizing races) plus two dogs, two lambs and the goat! Dave and the four children had tunics made of the fertilizer sacks; Dave's revealed his bony knees! They had hats made from the cut off corners of other sacks and Dave had made some plaits from sisal baler twine which stuck out from under his hat.

The lambs wore Union Jack coats as did the goat, but she also sported a fetching red hat with her ears poking through two appropriate slits. We had also made coats for the dogs who weren't very keen on them. Margaret and I just wore red skirts, blue jumpers and white hats; Lucy, the baby was in her colourfully decorated pram.

We walked along to the playing fields feeling rather silly but it was good fun.

Potatoes were grown each year and were harvested in October by anybody who was available. I tried it but discovered that I was more useful to look after children belonging to ladies who would rather pick potatoes. In the end it became a non-viable enterprise so was scrapped. A large acreage of corn was grown and when David had been working at the farm for six years, more land was bought about four miles from the main farm. This was very stony ground and when combining was attempted it was discovered that the crop had never been rolled at the appropriate time. It took weeks to cut the fields there and it was October before we could sing, "All is safely gathered in." A lot of the corn had to be dried down to the correct moisture content. This was mainly Dave's job and used to keep him busy until the early hours of the morning. It was a very dusty, dirty job as the dust found its way everywhere. As did a mouse which ran up Dave's trouser leg! He said that anyone watching him would have thought that he was doing a war dance as the poor mouse tried to make its escape.

Horses were also kept for the farmer's children to ride but unfortunately they often escaped from their field during the night. More than once Dave had to disappear into the night to chase the horses. In the end the problem was solved by putting padlocks on the gates. When the children no longer rode their ponies, they were used for 'Riding for the disabled'

8. A Change in the Air

Chapter 28

After thirteen years at the farm Dave felt like a change having improved the sheep flock and increased the corn output. The chance came when Dave heard that another farmer in the village needed a manager, as his son, who was to have helped, was going into a different industry. This was a smaller farm but as David knew the farmer quite well, he felt that there would be more of a challenge and also the opportunity to run a few sheep of his own. The boys would also be able to remain at their respective schools, Andrew was now at secondary school in Andover, and Peter was joining him later that year.

The farm was a young boy's delight with many barns full of interesting items of machinery. We moved into a sixteenth-century cottage which was extended for us and we spent several happy years there. The work was similar but there were a few other animals and assorted fowls and ducks. The boys had the chance as they grew older to learn to drive a tractor and help on the farm when they needed extra pocket money. When they were in their teens, they built up a flourishing summer holiday job, baling and carting bales. Andrew did the baling while Peter used a flat eight grab with great panache. They were in great demand in the neighbourhood and were able to each buy themselves a motor bike and later, when they went to college and university, to finance themselves.

There were about eight hundred breeding ewes, these were a breed known as North Country mules and were a cross-breed. The Suffolk ram was used on these although at one time Dave experimented with Texel rams that were becoming popular. The Suffolk seemed to produce the better lambs for meat which were what was needed. Lambing time was still very hectic but the farm staff all joined in so there was quite a good rota system which worked well unless the weather was bad. Our kitchen was always busy with cold soggy lambs in residence in the bottom oven of the Rayburn. Once they were on their feet I insisted that they went out in the barn.

We also had the help of various people on a very part time basis the most notable of which was 'The Colonel'. He was a retired Army officer and passionate about sheep. "Some folk take up golf, Eileen, and others go for bowls, but my hobby is sheep!" he told me one day as we walked together in the pouring rain across a wet, muddy field. His chief delight was to help with a 'real' flock of sheep, as although he possessed twenty-five of his own, he loved to get with the several hundred that Dave dealt with. He would often take charge of the lambing field while we had a meal as it was much easier if I could feed everyone together. On returning to the field one afternoon, I found the Colonel with a ewe upended before him trying valiantly to replace intestines into her.

"I'm sure I can get these back Eileen, everything came out as she was straining. The lambs are still inside her." I knew that a uterus could be replaced but not burst intestines.

"Well, Colonel, I really think that it's a job for Dave. Put some water on to boil while I go and find him".

He lowered the ewe to the ground, "Do you think so?" he asked quite relieved to be free of the responsibility and lit up his pipe gratefully.

I returned five minute later with Dave who obviously could do nothing but put the sheep down but he managed to save one of the two lambs she was carrying.

The rest of the farm staff were often pressed into service as sometimes there would be a sudden surge of lambs. Paul, the tractor driver was seventeen with no real experience of lambing. Dave had impressed on him that if a lamb wasn't breathing when it was born; the best thing was to swing it round by its hind legs. I was with Paul one day when he tried it. The wet lamb shot straight out of his hands into the air but Paul managed to field it nicely; I think he was used to playing cricket.

Dave tried to foster any orphan or rejected lambs if he could, but inevitably, there was nearly always one or two lambs that had to be bottle-fed. We became quite attached to some of them, one in particular was born on Easter Sunday was very weak and small but such an attractive lamb. Dave decided to call her 'Miriam'. She was very tame and when she grew into a ewe, Dave tried breeding from her. She made a rotten mother! We've discovered that most 'pet' lambs are the same; they just can't seem to relate to being mothers. We have learnt, however, that they are perfect for acting as flock leaders, they will follow Dave and the rest of the flock follow. Miriam was our first flock leader, we found her a cow-bell to wear around her neck on a dog collar, and she thought it was wonderful. When David led the flock through villages, she marched behind him, keeping on the white line in the middle of the road. One problem that became more apparent as time went on was that people moving into the village, cultivated the verges outside their houses and dispensed with gates! Dave used to drive along his planned route closing gates and trying to anticipate any likely hazards, but there was not much he could do about the 'open plan' gardens. The sheep often discovered that flowers tasted nicer than grass!

Miriam did suffer from a mistaken identity; she wasn't sure whether she was sheep, dog, or human. She loved to help

Dave eat his lunch, and would also eat the dog food from the sack when Dave made up the dogs' suppers. She also discovered that the dogs didn't always clear up their suppers, so when they left their raised kennels in the morning, she would stand on her hind legs to clear up what remained.

She also had a starring role in a Nativity play. Peter was in the Christian Union when he attended Surrey University at Guildford and they decided to perform an open-air Nativity play – using real animals. Andrew volunteered to drive Miriam to Guildford but was unable to use the Land Rover so had to take her in the Ford Escort that he drove at that time. He removed the front passenger seat and called Miriam who thought it was a wonderful idea to travel in style. She stood there. Chin resting on the dashboard, staring at the lights of approaching cars. Eventually they reached the University and Andrew managed to locate Peter.

"Bring Miriam over here Andrew."

Andrew attached her dog lead and she happily followed him along the path. They could see the lights and there were a lot of people milling around. Miriam wasn't so sure of this but Andrew kept talking to her so she went where he led.

"Can you get her to stand over there please Andrew? Would she let Colin lead her on?"

Miriam was wonderful and even the scruffy looking donkey and the other ewe which was led on didn't seem to worry her.

It was time to begin. Everyone settled in their 'seats' which were steps leading into the courtyard.

"And there was in the same country, shepherds keeping watch over their flock by night."

The Nativity play had begun.

Minty was another memorable sheep. She wasn't one of ours really but came to live with us when she was a few months old. A 'townie' had bought her as a pet for her young children but had little idea about sheep. The first thing she did was to give her a bath, thus washing away the natural oils in her wool. She treated her like a dog, bringing her indoors and settling her by the fire. Her children, being under five, weren't particularly interested in Minty, and her husband was furious when she ate the cabbages he had so carefully planted! In the end she had to go so joined us with the understanding that she wouldn't end up with mint sauce for Sunday lunch. Her full name *was* Mint Sauce! She was very spoilt but soon settled down and realized that she was a sheep and enjoyed living with the other 'pet' lambs.

Once the lambs were born there was then the problem of keeping them alive. Sometimes the problem was with the ewe that might have difficulties in feeding it. Lotty, a ewe that had been a bottle fed lamb a few years previously, had very short legs, a large udder and big lambs!

Dave came in one morning for breakfast,

"Lotty's lambs are having difficulties and although I've tried to make them kneel down to suckle, they just can't manage it. If I could just raise her udder in some way I think they'd soon get the right idea. Once they've sucked for a bit, her udder would be smaller. The only thing I can think of is a bra. Have you got an old one I could have?"

"Dave! Mine would never fit her. Still, if you think it will help I'll see what I can find."

I found one that had seen better days and Dave cut two strategic holes in it and tied it on her with baler twine.

"Lotty's feeding her lambs well now dear, thanks a lot. I'll buy you a new bra if you like."

Another problem lamb Dave brought home had broken back legs. It was a fine lamb so he set the bones and plastered them to stop them from moving. The lamb seemed quite content to lay in the sunshine and have a bottle every four hours. After a few weeks Dave took the plaster off.

"Eileen, that lamb's muscles are weak. I think it needs some sort of a baby bouncer fixed up to strengthen them. I thought that if you had a pair of knickers you didn't want, I could put its front legs through one leg and its back legs through the other hole. I could then tie string to the top and fix it to the washing line."

I exploded, "You've had my bra and now you want my knickers, what next will you ask for?"

We didn't notice immediately, our elderly spinster neighbour was creeping away from the back door which was wide open!--

The idea didn't work, the lamb obviously suffered from brittle bones and broke a front leg as soon as Dave suspended it -in my knickers- and he had to destroy it. I had to throw away my knickers!!

Chapter 29

Sheep weren't the only things that had problems at lambing time. There are diseases known as 'zoonoses' that are transmissible to humans. I went to the doctor.

"It's orf," he pronounced studying my thumb, "Have you been handling the sheep?"

The practice nurse was puzzled." How can it be off, it's still there?"

The doctor patiently explained the difference between 'orf' and 'off', as he farmed in his spare time he was familiar with the unusual name.

I had a feeling that was what it was as I had had it some years before. The correct name of 'orf' is 'contagious pustular dermatitis' so you can see why it is known by a shorter name!

It is an occupational hazard of rearing baby lambs as it appears around a lamb's mouth and is easily transmissible from there to hands. I thought I had been so careful about washing my hands but it doesn't take much to catch it. The symptoms are a very red, painful sore on the fingers but it can be transferred to the face, especially the lips. We had both had it one year soon after we were married when Dave had a delivery of sheep that he discovered were badly infected. There is no real cure for it and it has to take its course but it is a painful experience. It can take a more virulent form and produce 'flu like symptoms that can last for up to a year.

A few months later I was at the doctor's surgery again with my hand bandaged.

"Not orf again I hope?" the doctor sighed.

"Not this time doctor. I've managed to jab myself with a hypodermic needle!"

I unwound the bandage around my now, very swollen hand.

"However did you manage that?" queried the doctor, knowing that I never gave injections to the sheep.

"I was showing someone how the new self sterilizing syringe worked and held it against my hand and pushed the plunger by mistake. It was empty though."

The doctor looked at my hand; the puncture mark was barely visible.

"What product did the syringe have in it last?"

Thankfully I had thought to take the bottle of vaccine with me to show the doctor.

He decided to 'phone the firm that manufactured it to ask their advice as sheep medicines can cause problems.

"They think you must be allergic to the sterilizing agent as the actual product shouldn't cause any problems. You'll need an anti-histamine injection and also a course of anti-biotics as the needle had been used in a sheep."

David had an industrial accident once when he was doing a shearing demonstration at a village fete. He enjoyed these occasions when he could amaze people with the skills he had acquired over many years, he also managed to do a running commentary on what he was doing which people found fascinating. It was a lovely warm day, just right for shearing as the lanolin in the wool 'rises' and the cutters just glide through the fleece. He was getting on well spurred on by the appreciative 'Aahs' from the crowd as he held up the shorn fleece. He was on his sixth sheep when she became restless, the cutters missed the sheep and suddenly blood appeared to the horror of the crowd, who could only see the sheep and the blood. With great presence of mind, Dave grabbed the microphone, "Don't worry I haven't cut the sheep, it's my blood you can see."

A sigh of relief went up from the anxious spectators. Dave hastily finished shearing the sheep then made a bee-line for the first aid tent. He had run the cutters into his arm which was bleeding profusely. The nurse bandaged it for him but a few days later an infection developed and he had to have a course of anti-biotics.

Chapter 30

David had a 'phone call one day from the BBC.

"Mr. Sullivan, we want to make an 'Animal Magic' programme about sheep with Johnny Morris. We've heard that you are shepherd to several hundred sheep, Could you teach Johnny about lambing please?"

The crew arrived and surveyed the field where the lambing pens were set up in rows of ten, five each side of a gangway.

These in turn were either side of a wider gangway, altogether there were a hundred pens plus ten separate foster pens where ewes could be yoked. The lighting gang arrived and fixed up a big floodlight on top of a ten foot pole so that they could film some shots in the evening. Eventually, after everything was organised, the day came for Johnny Morris to arrive. We had permission for the boys to have time off school so they busied themselves cleaning out pens and being generally useful. Dave had to show Johnny step by step how to do each task which was repeated until he felt that he was competent enough. Then it was "Action" and the cameras rolled. It took a whole day and into the next to cover all the operations from Johnny 'delivering' a lamb, and getting it to suck. Then it had to have the necessary rubber rings applied to testicles and tail plus the iodine on its navel. The ewe had to be checked over, fed and watered after which on the 'next' day led out to the nursery field. The previous day's lambs were moved into a different field after making sure they were all sucking properly. It was an interesting two days and David was able to keep the floodlight for the rest of lambing.

We were all glued to the television when the programme was shown but were disappointed as apart from an introduction, Dave wasn't on and it was made to appear as if Johnny Morris had done everything unaided.

It is always difficult when ewes lamb in the field to persuade them to move into a pen. They have a tendency to follow their lamb or lambs which Dave carries in front of them, quite well, right to the entrance of the pen and then turn and bolt away. They need to be able to smell their lambs all the way, some shepherds hold the lambs by their front legs so that they dangle down but Dave doesn't like that method. He drew plans for a 'lamb pram' and took it to the local blacksmith for his suggestions.

"Yes, I think I could make that. How long do you want the handle Dave?"

"I should think about three foot, with a rubber grip so I don't lose hold of it."

Dave picked it up a week later. It was just how he had planned it about eighteen inches off the ground similar to an open topped cage on wheels and he was longing to try it out.

It was marvellous and revolutionised bringing in the lambs as the ewe could keep her nose right on the lamb and walked behind the pram. The pram was also used on occasions in a reverse way if a ewe was 'scatty' or nervous when Dave would seat her unceremoniously in the pram and tuck the lamb under his arm.

Chapter 31

We tried to go away each year for a holiday with the boys and one particular week we had planned to go to Cumbria where some friends had offered us the use of a small chalet on a private site. It was in a small village on the coast, Allonby, not far from Cockermouth. We had to take Briar with us who was about ten years old by this time and semi-retired. We left our other dog, Jan, behind as she would be needed for any necessary sheep work. Briar loved the beach and the waves but wasn't keen on the sea as it tasted funny. There were several thunderstorms while we were there and Briar had always been terrified of them. If we were in the car, he'd try and crawl under our legs and in the chalet he'd worm his way under the bed.

Once when we were at home I was outside in the yard when there was a sudden flash of lightning and rumble of thunder. Hearing a noise, I looked up to see Briar poised on the upstairs bathroom windowsill about to jump! I shouted at him and ran upstairs just in time to stop him. Usually he could sense when a storm was coming becoming increasingly distressed, salivating excessively and shaking like a leaf. If one occurred during the night, one of us would have to sit with him until it was over. We tried having him upstairs with us but at every crash of thunder, he'd complete a circuit of the bedroom without touching the floor.

He slept in the chalet on the floor but as soon as Dave got up to make a cup of tea, he'd lay outside in the little garden and watch the world go by. We had planned to stay for the weekend with a friend in Carlisle before heading south on the Monday as we were going to the Royal Show at Stoneleigh.

On the Saturday morning, Briar went out as usual and I was still in bed waiting for Dave to bring my usual cup of tea when I heard a dog bark a little way off. It sounded familiar.

"Dave, where's Briar?"

"Outside as usual."

"Are you sure because that sounded very much like his bark?"

Dave went to check.

"He's gone, the gate's open. He can't have gone far; I'll go and look for him."

I dressed quickly. The boys and I had our breakfast. An hour later Dave came back looking worried, "I can't find him anywhere, I've whistled and called him but he's vanished. Somebody did see him running away from another dog so he could be miles away by now. I think I'll just go and tell the policeman in case anyone 'phones."

"Good morning. Can I help you?" The policeman looked up expectantly.

"I hope so," replied Dave, "I've lost a dog....."

The policeman pulled a block of forms towards him. "Could you give me some details please?" He noted down all Dave's necessary details and then started on Briar's. "What breed?"

"Border Collie".

"Colour?"

"Black and white".

The policeman looked up in amusement. Every other dog in Cumbria was a black and white Border Collie.

"Age?"

"Ten, I think."

"Any distinguishing features?"

"Yes, he has half a tongue and half a tail and leers lopsidedly.—

The policeman started writing it down.

Dave continued, "The half of his tail that's missing is the back half!"

The policeman started writing that down too then burst out laughing.

"Well there can't be many dogs with that description. I'll ring Maryport and let them know and they'll issue a general search. Come and see me later and I'll let you know how we've got on."

David took the boys and me to our friend at Carlisle and after a meal returned to Allonby promising to return in the morning. He slept in the car and toured all the farms in the area early next morning, catching farmers milking their cows, thinking someone may have seen him. The dog seemed to have totally disappeared. We all spent the afternoon at Allonby and decided, after further consultation with the policeman, to get in touch with Radio Carlisle who appealed for missing persons at lunchtime on Mondays.

The morning was wet, as only mornings in Cumbria can be. There was a cattle market in Cockermouth so we decided to spend the morning there. There were three separate rings for sheep, pigs and cows. Dave suddenly had an idea.

"Have you got any sheets of paper and a pen?"

"Well, I've got a pen – here, will this paper do?"

"Just the job".

Dave scribbled something down and disappeared into the crowd.

"There, that might help. I've given Briar's details to all three auctioneers to announce."

We were by the sheep ring when Dave's notice was read out.

"Has anyone seen a black and white border collie? Lost at Allonby on Saturday. Distinguishing features; only has half a tail and half a tongue. Please contact the police station at Allonby."

We listened to the same message on the car radio at twelve o'clock.

"We'd better go back to Allonby now and load the canoe on the car," said Dave as we had been able to leave it there.

We were just tying the last rope when we heard a shout,

"He's been seen," and there, running through the driving rain towards us in his shirtsleeves was the policeman. "I'm glad I've caught you although I had put a message out to the motorway patrols to watch out for you." He had a map with him and showed us where Briar had been seen, a farm about fifteen miles away. We thanked him profusely and promised to let him know the outcome. Driving as fast as the narrow lanes would allow we soon covered the fifteen miles. As we drove into the farmyard, a man came out to meet us.

"Are you looking for the dog with half a tongue and half a tail? I tried to catch him but he ran off in that direction. I've 'phoned the people at the next village and they're looking out for him."

Exmoor 1957. David in 'Sunday best'.
[Photo: South Molton Photographers]

Mr. Hatt's farm 1956. David showing off the bull.
[Photo: Eileen Sullivan]

Romney Marsh Shearing Championship 1961. David shearing in under 21 competition – he won! [Photo: Eileen Sullivan]

East Brabourne 1959 Rosie; the first sheepdog of many. [Photo: Eileen Sullivan]

Hurstbourne Tarrant 1977. The Family (including pets!) celebrating the Queen's Silver Jubilee. [Photo: Eileen Sullivan]

Hurstbourne Tarrant 1976. Sheep moving early Sunday morning on Hurstbourne Hill. [Photo: David Sullivan]

Faccombe 1985. David showing his sheepdogs.
[Photo: The Sheep Farmer]

Hurstbourne Tarrant 1982. David posing for the media
before going to the Antipodes. [Photo: Newbury Weekly News]

Illustrations for Nuffield report by Guy Cawton

Hurstbourne Tarrant 1988. David's plan for handling rams. [Photo: Farmer's Weekly]

Stitchcombe 1994. Sheep being dipped in mobile sheep dip. [Photo: John Burrows]

Stitchcombe 1994. Sheep draining after being dipped. [Photo: John Burrows]

Hurstbourne Tarrant 1998. Danny, Dilly, and their babies. [Photo: Eileen Sullivan]

Hurstbourne Tarrant 2000. Revived lamb escaping from the oven before it's too late! [Photo: Eileen Sullivan]

Hurstbourne Tarrant. 2002. Relaxing at home. [Photo: Lily Frampton]

Lynmouth 2002. One man and his dog.... on holiday. [Photo: Eileen Sullivan]

Hurstbourne Tarrant 2003. Showing shorn fleece at school Fete. [Photo: Andover Advertiser]

Hurstbourne Tarrant 2004. "Little Lamb, who made thee?" [Photo: Eileen Sullivan]

Hurstbourne Tarrant 2005. David with Pip and Bud. [Photo: Lorna Butler]

Hurstbourne Tarrant 2006. Sheep and lambs [Photo: George Purver]

Hurstbourne Tarrant 2007. Pip on front lawn enjoying his retirement. [Photo: Eileen Sullivan]

We shouted our thanks and continued our search. As we drove into the village there was a group of people with umbrellas,

"Have you seen..." we began, and they finished "...a dog with half a tongue and half a tail. Yes we have but he went that way, about five minutes ago."

We were definitely getting nearer our objective. We saw a man coming from a lane on a bike.

"Have you seen a black and white collie around?"

"With half a tongue and half a tail? He's in a field down that lane but he wouldn't let me get near him."

"Thanks" we shouted winding the windows up and indicating right. We stopped a hundred yards along the lane and jumped out. "Briar!" we all shouted. There, dragging a rabbit carcase across the field was our lost dog, wet, bedraggled and confused. Hearing our shout he let go of the carcase and started running – away from us.

"Shh!" said Dave and he put his fingers in his mouth and gave the "Walk up" whistle. Briar stopped running and looked round. "Here Briar" called Dave softly. The old dog came across the field, stump wagging slowly as he tried to take it in. He wasn't lost any more. We made such a fuss of him – he was even given half a chocolate cake to eat, his tins of dog food were at the bottom of the boot, we dried our tears of joy and settled down. We found a big bath towel to spread over the boys' knees and drove off with a wet, smelly, but so happy, dog across it.

He suffered no ill effects from his experience but he retired after this (although he would sometimes decide to help Dave in the sheep pens across the other side of the road) and lived until the age of twelve, learning a whole lot of new skills as he became a house dog. He enjoyed travelling in the car, especially when it was shopping day and he could sit proudly in the back seat and bark at any dog that dared to pass the car in the car park.

He learnt when it was my baking morning and would sit as near me as he could and wait for any scraps that might fall to the floor. He died peacefully from a stroke at the age of twelve. Dave buried him beneath the sheep pens!

Chapter 32

Before Briar died, we had bought a replacement for him, Jill. She was a puppy from Cumbria a registered sheep dog, Dave bought her with the hope of breeding his own dogs and a couple of years later he decided to buy a dog pup who inevitably was named Jack. We had arranged to travel to Wales to collect him but had no car at the time. Friends were going near the farm in Wales so volunteered to bring him back with them.

"Phew! We had to drive all the way with the windows down. It smells as if he'd been kept in a chicken shed."

He looked a pathetic little thing and scratched continually. When we examined him closer, his skin was red and raw. We put him in the utility room sink which was quite deep, found some dog shampoo and gave him a good bath. At least he smelled a bit better although his skin was still sore. Dave rang his previous owner to ask about the skin condition.

"The best thing to clear that is cabbage water. I've been giving it to him for the last couple of weeks! If you're not satisfied with him you can bring him back."

There was no way we were going to let him return to whatever conditions he had been kept in so we persevered with daily baths until he was rid of all the mites that he was covered in. He grew rapidly but unfortunately, showed no interest in sheep, in fact, he tended to be wary of them. His main interest in life was cars! When he was supposed to be in the sheep pens he'd be found at the bottom of the lane watching the traffic. His chief delight was travelling in a car looking at all the traffic passing on the other side of the road. In time he fathered five puppies, one of which had a deformed mouth so had to be put down. The other four were fun to watch and Jill proved to be a really devoted mother but she'd take time off now and again to be a sheep dog if she heard Dave working in the pens across the road. We advertised the puppies and sold three of them to good homes but kept Ben for ourselves. We heard about one bitch for some years afterwards as his owner kept us in touch with her exploits, although she wasn't used as a sheepdog, Pepsi became a champion in agility trials. It became apparent that Jack was never going to be a sheep dog although he was very obedient and had a nice nature. A friend needed a cattle dog, and, surprisingly, Jack didn't mind cows so it was agreed that he'd go for a month's trial period and if he proved to be satisfactory then we'd sell him. Unfortunately, we received a 'phone call three weeks later.

"Dave, I'm so sorry, Jack's dead. He was in the yard with some cows and one of them must have kicked him. There was nothing I could do."

It was decided that Dave would receive half the agreed price.

By this time Ben was beginning to work nicely. He was a gentle dog and very good with ewes and lambs as some dogs can be aggressive, and try to move them too quickly. This scatters the flock causing ewes to lose lambs which tend to become panic stricken when they can't find their Mums. He had the endearing habit of taking a hand in his mouth when he was not working and we were walking along. He lived until he was about four years old then had an accident, falling out of the back of the Land Rover into the path of an oncoming car. Since then, Dave has had the back of the Land Rover equipped with a secure metal mesh gate so it becomes a portable dog kennel.

Chapter 33

David often moved sheep by walking them along the road. He always walked in front with the dogs coming behind the flock. Sometimes he'd move them for two or three miles as there were some fields on different farms. This could cause traffic problems although he tried to move them when the roads weren't too busy, early Sunday morning was the best time. Some motorists became very impatient on rounding a bend and being confronted by a large flock of sheep. Nothing annoyed Dave more than motorists either trying to push by them or keeping their finger on the horn. He finally solved the problem however.......

Working in the farm office was the most attractive girl, Sally. She was very versatile and could turn her hand to most things, even shearing – in a pair of short shorts and bikini top – but always looked immaculate the next morning. She had a friend, Jane, also young and attractive.

Sally walked in front of the sheep while Jane walked behind with the dogs – there were no more complaints after that. The local paper even took a photograph of them with the sheep entitling it, "Bo-Peeps and their sheep". The police sometimes turned up and drove in front with their blue light flashing.

"They never did that when I led them," protested Dave who would follow the entourage in his van a few cars behind the sheep.

The boys went on to the local sixth form college to take 'A' levels, and each bought a motor bike on which to get to

Andover. Dave realised what a useful vehicle it was and bought one too. The boys passed their motorbike riding test with no bother. Dave failed. He had insisted that the boys had lessons and learnt to ride their bikes properly but didn't doubt that *he'd* pass. At the age of forty, he joined the class along with teenage boys, much to their delight, and dutifully followed the instructor as they traversed the side roads of Andover. He had more delight in passing that test than the one for driving a car.

Dave came in a bit late one evening, looking a bit dazed.

"Whatever's the matter?" I queried.

"I fell off my motor bike on the way home. I think I dozed off and hit a drainage ditch at the side of the road."

"How did you get home? Where were you?" I pushed him into the armchair as he didn't look too good.

I was coming along Netherton Bottom and I came home on the motor bike."

One of the boys went outside to look at the bike. "Dad, the handlebars are completely twisted to one side, I don't know how you managed to steer it properly!"

After a good night's sleep he didn't seem to have any ill effects and gave the motor bike a good overhaul.

Dave came in for breakfast.

"Could you take Jill to the vet for me, Eileen? She seems to have hurt her leg."

The vet examined her.

"She seems to have damaged it in some way, I'd better have her X-rayed." Has she been hit by a car or something?"

"I don't think so. Dave didn't say anything if she had."

"Well, leave her here and telephone later."

I reached the car when I suddenly remembered and rushed back, Bursting into the consulting room to the amazement of the owner of the dog just being examined.

"I've just remembered, Jill fell off the motor bike a few days ago!"

I explained to the amused vet that David had been to look at some sheep in a location that could only be reached on foot or on the motor bike. He had to travel along a very rutted track and the inevitable happened. – He fell off. – As he was only wearing shorts and working boots he was quite bruised, but no bones broken. Jill, the dog was riding pillion and was most upset to find herself on the ground.

The dog was just bruised and recovered after a few days rest.

I had to take Andrew to the doctor a few weeks later with a damaged hand.

"I managed to get my fingers jammed in a centipede!"

The doctor lived in the village and his parents were farmers, so he knew that a centipede was a 'tedder' and had many legs; hence its name.

9. The Nuffield Experience

Chapter 34

In 1980 a farming friend suggested that David should apply for a Nuffield Farming Scholarship. The scholarships were inaugurated by the Nuffield Foundation to enable suitable applicants to travel and study farming subjects abroad. Dave thought about it and as the upper age limit was forty, which he would be in under a year, decided to apply. His chosen subject was "The Human Factor in Sheep Farming" which he wanted to study in New Zealand and Australia. He felt it would make an interesting study and one that had not been researched as sheep farming wasn't in the forefront of agriculture. There were often articles in the Farmers Weekly about sheep – different breeds, ways of keeping sheep etc. but nothing about the needs of the shepherds and their aspirations.

After completing the application form and sending that and his C.V. he was eventually invited to an interview in London. This was quite intimidating and took place in an office near Regents Park. He was ushered into a room with about ten men sitting around a huge boardroom type table, and was asked to sit in a chair placed at one end so took his seat with some trepidation. Questions asked by the men, Dave found were not as onerous as he had anticipated. As his interests outside farming were asked about on the application form, David had mentioned his involvement with the Gospel Hall and also his lay preaching. This caused one comment as to why he thought it was right for him to stand up in front of others and give his opinion on these matters. Dave was able to answer to the gentleman's satisfaction as one of the qualifications for the scholarship was the ability to pass on the knowledge that was gained.

He was offered the scholarship and left for the Antipodes in December 1982 having planned a tour of Australia and New Zealand aiming to return in February 1983. I stayed at home with the boys. Andrew was due to take 'A' levels in the summer and Peters 'O' levels were also taking place at the same time so it didn't seem the right time for me to go abroad, we couldn't afford it in any case. All David's expenses were met by the Trust and quite an extensive itinerary was planned. It was the first time that David had been anywhere by 'plane and he was looking forward to the experience. He went to sleep quite quickly after boarding as there had been so much to sort out to cater for his absence while he would be away. Awaking some hours later, he felt rather hungry so caught the attention of a stewardess.

"Is there any chance of a meal please?"

The stewardess smiled, "Dinner was two hours ago, we tried to wake you. Would some sandwiches be all right?"

David began to enjoy the flight and even had the opportunity to visit the flight deck which he found very interesting. After the 'plane stopped at Singapore, David changed his seat, sitting between an Australian and an Asian lady who was wearing typical concealing black clothing The space in front of her was filled with bags and brown paper parcels. Her legs seemed to be non existent until David sat down and felt what seemed to be a foot against his thigh; she was sitting cross legged on the seat!

After about an hour came a warning that there was some turbulence ahead and to fasten safety belts. The lady didn't seem to understand and as she made no movement, Dave thought he'd better help her. He discovered eventually that she was sitting on her belt! It was quite bumpy for about ten minutes but it was too long for Dave's companion and she reached for her sick bag. One wasn't enough however, and Dave found that he had to find a lot more for her.

There was a dearth of stewardesses just then so David had to deal with the bags after she had used them! Then the trolley appeared with the dinner. She insisted on having one although Dave tried to indicate to her that it might not be a good idea. It wasn't, especially when accompanied by coca cola! Dave was kept busy again but nothing spoilt his appetite and he ate her sweet as well as his own.

Chapter 35

Eventually he arrived in Australia where he was to spend two weeks before travelling to Tasmania for a week and then to New Zealand. Australia was in the middle of a drought and as Dave travelled around to various farms he saw at first hand the terrible effect it had. Some farmers had had to slaughter their flocks and herds at a great loss. The farmers had various ingenious ways of conserving what water fell in other seasons of the year. Corrugated iron roofs conducted rain water into tanks which was then channelled into other holding tanks further down the hills. These could then be led into troughs but there was still never quite enough. Use was made of the topography so rain ran off was caught by earth dams and ponds were the result. The sheep appeared to be kept on bare earth but the farmer showed Dave that in the soil were seeds – weeds mainly and the animals were grubbing them out.

David also had the unforgettable experience of shearing with an Australian sheep shearing gang, one of the highlights of his tour. It's a highly organised operation, beginning early in the morning, continuing throughout the day. The sheep are shorn in strictly regulated two hour 'runs' with fifteen minutes allowed for a 'smoko' before starting again. The shearers shear on one level, the shorn sheep are put down chutes and run out underneath the shed. The wool hands are on the next level and throw the fleeces on to circular tables for sorting and classing. The wool is then dumped into bins to one side of the floor and on the ground floor a man presses the wool into a hydraulic press and bales it. David found the merino sheep with their loose folds of skin much harder to shear than the mules that he was used to in England.

The farming methods generally were totally different from those in Great Britain. There is much more land but less grass for the sheep and they live on small seeds in pods of subterranean clover. The food value of them is very high and the sheep looked well although the Australian Merino is not one of the best looking sheep.

David spent three days in Tasmania. The first day he spent working with a gang who were performing a number of tasks on a huge 'mob' of lambs, one thousand. These lambs had been weaned so were a few months old. After being herded into holding pens, they were driven through a race to a sort of roundabout contraption upon which the lamb was hoisted on to its back with its hind legs in a clamp, presenting its rear end to the operator at waist height. The 'roundabout' was operated by a foot pedal and the lamb moved round to the next position. They were castrated by rubber rings, tailed with a hot iron, and sprayed with fly spray by different operators at each stopping point but the second job that was done was 'meusling'. This was an operation that would not be allowed in this country on the grounds that it was cruel. It is done by a skilled operator and consists of cutting off strips of skin around the vaginal and anal area. This is for cleanliness purposes as there is a bad blow fly problem in Tasmania. The flesh heals quickly and stretches the bare area and makes it bigger than it was, rather like a 'face lift' only at the other end!

Another operation that is performed is tailing by hot iron and castration by rubber ring which in England both jobs are done by rubber rings when the lambs are a day old. The roundabout made for a very slick operation and by lunch time 500 lambs had been processed. They had been vaccinated, ear tagged, muesled, castrated, tailed, and fly sprayed. It was a very gory procedure altogether, as after the muesling there was quite a lot of blood around. Everything was on huge scale with shearing sheds built for 1000 sheep on a slatted floor and involved sheep races and holding pens around the buildings.

On returning to Australia, one of the visits Dave made was to a farm where the sheep are housed all the time in individual pens in a big shed on slatted floors in order to produce a pure unadulterated product called 'Sharlea wool'. The wool is very fine, like silk, and destined for an Italian fashion house, it is worth five times the price as normal wool. No straw or other contaminants must spoil the wool.

Dave was able to visit many places in South Australia, Victoria, and New South Wales and received a welcome everywhere. He only stayed in three or four hotels during the whole trip and was offered hospitality everywhere else. A lot of houses have a guest suite as they're so remote that there isn't anywhere else to stay in any case. Part of the time in Australia he was able to spend with my sister Pam, who with her husband and children, emigrated to Melbourne in 1965.

On one of Dave's farm visits in Australia, he was taken to a wildlife park near Adelaide, it was the only place in Australia that he saw kangaroos with 'joeys' in their pouches, koalas, wombats and the colourful parakeets were also in evidence. Not all of Dave's visits were to farms and he spent some time talking to people involved in man management and various firms. The lack of history in Australia came as a surprise to him. We lived in a sixteenth century house and he was proudly shown buildings that were a hundred years old which were considered really ancient.

The autonomy that the shepherds had in caring for their sheep was different to the way that things were done in England. There was much more freedom and incentive in Australia to improve the stock and handling of the sheep.

Chapter 36

On Christmas Eve, Dave flew to New Zealand and spent some time with his sister in Auckland before going to stay with friends, Nigel and Marion for a week over Christmas. He went to a midnight service in Auckland and found it strange to be wearing shorts and short sleeved shirt singing 'In the bleak mid winter'.

Nigel and Marion lived near the beach with their large family who either lived at home or nearby. There are no building restrictions in New Zealand so as each child arrived Nigel created another bedroom in the roof with low passages between them. A new experience for David was sailing which he greatly enjoyed as the weather was good, and New Zealand has a similar climate to Spain.

He visited Rotorua with its thermal springs and geysers, all appropriately named – 'Hell's Gate' was one of them. Warning signs were everywhere, as to stray off the path could be fatal as on each side were deep bubbling pools of mud. There was an unbearable stench of sulphur in the air which made breathing quite difficult. A lot of the buildings in the area were heated by thermal springs and Dave spent time in a swimming pool also heated in this way which was the temperature of a bath. Near Rotorua he spent a couple of days staying at a camp for children which proved very interesting. "Kiwi Ranch" was one of several similar camps all over New Zealand; the youngsters were housed in log cabins containing about eight bunks. Everything was very basic but some of the activities available on the site although very ingenious would never be permitted in England!

There was a 'flying boat' consisting of a large canoe suspended from a long overhead cable that the children sat in and then travelled down a hill for about 100 yards. An old car was parked at the top of the slope and a rope around the back wheel acted as a winch to pull the boat up again. In the middle of a shallow lake was an upright pole secured in the bottom of the pool. It had four arms with car tyres suspended from each and these revolved using car engine power. The health and safety factor didn't seem to operate there as the chain pulleys were completely unguarded, attitude seemed to be that – 'the children must learn to be careful.' If they fell off into the water it would teach them to hold on tighter next time.

Another highlight of his tour was a visit to the Agrodome, which is an exhibition to demonstrate the sheep of New Zealand, also situated near Rotorua. It is a very impressive building, lined with wood, seating about three hundred people with a stage at one end.

Ivor Bowen (brother of Godfrey Bowen who taught Dave to shear when he was in Kent) introduced the performance. Rams walked on breed by breed with a taped commentary and each climbed on to a pedestal until nineteen rams were in a pyramid. Ivor meanwhile had changed and a shearing machine rose out of the floor in front of the audience. Ivan sheared a sheep at normal speed and then at a slow speed while he talked about the technique. He then explained about the wool and demonstrated how docile a sheep is in the hands of an expert.

Then a New Zealand Huntaway dog was introduced, various commands demonstrated and finally the dog climbed on the backs of the rams until it reached the magnificent merino ram at the apex of the pyramid where it sat proudly on its back. Afterwards Ivor worked three sheep with a collie 'eye' dog; the whole performance lasted about an hour. Even the children in the audience were spellbound and were able to make a fuss of the dogs. There was also a shop that sold all kinds of knitwear and sheepskin products which were snapped up by the Americans who were amongst several other nationalities who were in the audience. The goods that were bought could be shipped straight to anywhere in the world.

The exhibition was first thought of when the World Trade Fair was held in Japan a few years earlier. The Sheep presentation was New Zealand's exhibit. The sheep had to be housed on a ship from the New Zealand navy that was moored in the harbour. Each morning, the sheep, after being groomed were taken to the exhibition site by ratings from the ship, accompanied by the band. The sailors were very proud to have the honour of leading these magnificent animals and crowds of people lined the streets of Tokyo to watch the procession.

Dave spent that night with Ivor and his wife, Joyce in their house on the shore of Lake Rotorua. He had a swim in the lake before dinner was eaten on the verandah overlooking the lake. As in many New Zealand houses there was a self-contained guest suite on the ground floor which Dave occupied.

A few days later, Dave was able to meet up again with Godfrey and Mavis, his wife. David heard that since he had learnt to shear with Godfrey, a lot had happened. Godfrey had literally shorn all over the world and been honoured in various places including Britain where he had received an

M.B.E. and U.S.S.R. where he was made a 'Hero of the Russian Empire' – and kissed on both cheeks by Kruschev!

Dave spent Sunday with Godfrey and Mavis and joined them in worship at the church they attended. He felt privileged to be introduced as 'My friend David from England.' Roast lunches aren't usual in New Zealand so he really enjoyed the one that Mavis had prepared. Barbeques seem to be the norm accompanied by lots of different salads with fish, which is plentiful, being high on the menu too.

Chapter 37

Dave then flew to Invercargill in South Island, which was rather different to the North Island. The country there was mountainous with snow on the tops and that was in their summer. It resembled Scotland in many ways. Many of the original settlers came from there and the general atmosphere was similar with place names being the same, Dunedin, Invercargill etc. A rental car had been arranged for him and he had a seventy-mile drive to his first visit. As he had done in Australia, he picked up hitchhikers whenever possible, he enjoyed company and it was the usual way for youngsters to travel around. The farming operations were more extensive than in the North Island, which was very relaxed. Deer farming was a new experience that at that time was not being done in England. The deer were initially caught in the wild being spotted by helicopters and on this particular farm the herd numbered 300 and was very profitable. The velvet from the antlers was used as an aphrodisiac and provided the major source of the farm income accounting for a third of the total income although occupying a very small section of the farm. If they needed handling, it was done in nearly dark conditions, as deer are very nervous animals.

There is a big problem with weeds, as the early settlers introduced plants native to Scotland that reminded them of home. Thistles and gorse are particular problems. Animals too were imported and, as there were no natural predators, have really got out of hand; wild deer and goats have destroyed thousands of acres of native forest as well as rabbits eating a lot of the grass. There are no snakes or reptiles of any kind and the authorities are anxious to keep it that way so imports and visitors are subjected to rigorous inspections.

Dave visited the Cattledrome which was near Queenstown and similar to the Agrodome in North Island. The cattle were on display in an open fronted shed, very tame and seemed to enjoy the attention paid to them by the children. The show started with a fifteen-minute film about New Zealand, followed by a taped commentary introducing the cattle breeds of the country. As each breed was introduced, they came in and climbed on to raised platforms and munched away at the food placed there. There were Hereford, Aberdeen Angus, Beef Shorthorn, Charollais, Simmental and Red Poll, beautifully groomed and in perfect condition. Then three dairy cows entered, Jersey, Friesian and Ayrshire. They took up positions on a roundabout in the centre of a stage and the Jersey cow was milked by machine. The audience was then invited to dip paper cups into the milk to sample the taste of milk direct from the cow. The invitation was then issued to try hand milking one of the other cows. If a 'milker' was able to squirt a bit of milk out of a teat they were awarded a certificate of 'udderance'. There was a great deal of camera flashing as children – and adults – were photographed in front of 'their' cow. There was a wide range of merchandise which must have been the major source of income as the entrance fees were very reasonable.

Dave spent some time with a delightful couple, Malcolm and Mona who lived in a suburb of Christchurch. Malcolm was the owner of a large building contracting firm although semi-retired as his sons had taken over the business. While Dave was there he visited their local church which they attended each week and found it similar to the Gospel Hall at home.

David stayed there three days and had the opportunity of taking to the water in a jet boat – this is driven by a turbine that drives a jet of water instead of using propeller. The New Zealand river was very shallow but there was no danger of damaging the non-existent propeller on the many rocks or shingle banks. Malcolm's son Selwyn drove the boat on the exciting trip up the river, achieving a speed of about forty miles per hour against a strong current, leaping shingle banks on the way. An even faster speed was reached on the return journey as the current helped. It was a very exciting trip as the river had many twists and turns. Selwyn was preparing for the round New Zealand Marathon boat race which was taking place later that year.

One night was spent at Malcolm and Mona's holiday home, or 'batch' at a place called 'Hammer Springs', which, as the name suggests, was another area of hot springs and pools. Dave and Malcolm spent an hour or so sitting in a pool that was as hot as a bath and very invigorating owing to the minerals in the water. They could admire the beautiful view as the house was situated in the hills. It was very well equipped and Dave played pool in the games room – another first for him.

The next day Dave had a drive of two hundred miles to get to the ferry which would take him back to North Island. When he reached Picton and found the ferry, he discovered there was an ingenious way for dealing with luggage as he had to leave the car there. Four lorries had racks for suitcases which were loaded by the owners, and then the lorries were driven on to the ferry and off the other end where the luggage was collected .

Chapter 38

Dave collected the Mini and spent a night with Godfrey and Mavis before heading off to a local Agricultural Show. It was similar to an English Show but with a big emphasis on wood chopping skills. In New Zealand there are axeman clubs and it is a national sport as it is also in Canada and Australia. One competition simulated felling a tree. A specially constructed stand had a log clamped to it in a vertical position; each axeman had a handicap according to his past competition records. A staggered start was designed to give the experts a handicap and make the contest more exciting.

"On your blocks," intoned the timekeeper, and a countdown began, counting the seconds so when a number was reached, each man could start and he made his first stroke. The experts started about fifteen seconds behind the first competitor. The first block to fall was the one declared the winner and presumably after winning some competitions the handicap was altered. Each log was connected by a 'string' to an overhead switch which broke an electrical circuit immediately the log was severed. The switches consisted of electric kettle sockets with a bent piece of metal stuck in each hole, which, when pulled down by the string broke the circuit and lit up an indicator light on the judges' console.

The most exciting competition was the 'jigger pole'. This involved a slot being cut in an vertical 'tree trunk' a board was inserted, the axeman then jumped up on it and cut another slot and this continued up to the top, then the top few feet had to be cut from the tree.

There was also a race between two men with a crosscut saw and a man using a chain saw – the crosscut saw won! The chain saw was only two thirds of the way through the log when the crosscut finished.

The saws and axes were beautifully maintained and kept in special hand made cases. The Maoris had lovely carvings on theirs and great pride was taken. The saws were hand made from sheets of flat steel with the teeth filed out to precise angles and if sold fetched high prices.

After a couple more farm visits and a brief stay at Maureen's, Dave flew back to Melbourne. He spent three days with my sister and spent the time collecting his thoughts together to begin writing up his Nuffield report. Eventually, he headed off to the airport and boarded the plane for the U.K. He settled in his seat and waited for take off. Suddenly the sky began to darken and the captain's voice issued from the loudspeaker.

"Please fasten your safety belts. We are taking off immediately as there is a dust storm approaching!"

As the plane taxied along the runway preparing for take off, at the edge of the airfield was a long, black, ground based cloud rolling towards the plane. Just when it appeared that they would run right into it the plane rose above it and they were airborne. It was a phenomenal sight and Dave managed to take some outstanding photographs of the dust cloud. Later he heard that theirs was the last aircraft to take off for some hours and the dust cloud had blacked out most of Melbourne.

After ten minutes flying, Dave became aware of a lot of activity among the cabin staff. They were taking the fire extinguishers out from their holders and some of the stewards started pulling off the ceiling panels. Once again the metallic voice from the loudspeaker was heard

"This is your captain speaking. There seems to be a small fire which members of staff are dealing with. We are going on to Sydney as Melbourne Airport is now closed owing to the dust storm. Please keep your seat belts fastened."

There were now drifts of acrid smoke wafting through the cabin. Dave closed his eyes and committed himself and the plane to God's mercy. He was amused by an elderly lady sitting in front of him who had been knitting since take off and continued without a break. Eventually, they reached Sydney without further mishap and transferred to another plane. After an eleven-hour flight, he eventually landed at Heathrow where Andrew and I were waiting for him. It took just over an hour to reach home and there, waiting to greet Dave, was the latest addition to the family – Larry the lamb, who had been born a bit prematurely so was wearing an old woolly jersey as his Mum had rejected him and he had to be kept warm.

Lambing started earlier than planned so Dave was plunged straight back into work and suffered badly from jetlag.

"Sorry dear, I'm not hungry". He'd then curl up on the settee after work and sleep all evening until I awoke him to go to bed. He had always had the gift of being able to go to sleep easily – at any time and in any place regardless of circumstances and it hasn't changed over the years.

Chapter 39

On one occasion we had taken a party of teenagers away for a weekend to a 'barn camp' and on the Saturday Dave was officiating at a wedding twenty miles away. He had had little sleep on the Friday night; I drove to the wedding while he dozed. The wedding went off without a hitch but Dave amused everybody at the reception especially the bride, by dozing off between courses. However, the maitre d'hotel took a different view and was not amused; Dave received a very rude awakening with a vigorous slap across his shoulders, thirty five years later the bride and groom still remind him of the event whenever they meet him.

Dave was now busier than ever as he was invited to speak about his trip to the Antipodes to various groups. He had amassed slides of his journeys which he collated into a comprehensive collection that he was able to vary for the different types of audience. These ranged from Women's' Institutes to the Nuffield Farming Conference at the Waldorf Hotel in London.

This was a very impressive gathering, wives were invited as well, (I found this intimidating and was totally out of my depth). Dave had to present his report on "The Human Factor in Sheep Farming". All the other Nuffield Scholars who had been awarded scholarships in 1983/4 also had their reports to present, for which they were each allocated fifteen minutes. They were also given another fifteen minutes for questions and some of the prominent people in the agricultural world were there.

David had asked my nephew, Guy, in Australia, to draw a number of cartoons illustrating the various aspects of his subject that he wanted covered. He had them made into transparencies for use with an overhead projector and used them with great effect as he spoke. I was more nervous than he was, and was glad when he had finished but it was obvious by the questions that were fired at him that he had made an impression. Some of the ideas were quite revolutionary, such as sheep share farming, which he was later able to put into practice. He also investigated the motivations for shepherding – he had conducted a survey amongst shepherds for this. – He also had his own theory of the Archimedes principle (about the displacement of water) that fitted in with his sheep ideas. His report, of which 100 copies were printed, actually had to be reprinted as the years passed. He found it hard to resume 'normal' work again, but, as usual, events occurred to enliven the situation.

Every year in the autumn the annual Nuffield Farming Scholarship conference was held in different parts of the country when the returning scholars read out their reports. These events took place over two days with a dinner on the first evening and usually a tour of whichever city in which the conference was held, before concluding. Wives were invited as well and as they were held in top class hotels, often with swimming pools, we quite enjoyed the trips. I didn't sit through all the reports but could go window shopping. One year when the event was held in Durham, we joined a tour of the city arranged by the organizers, which included the cathedral. There was a service in place and to our amazement; the speaker was Terry Waite who hadn't been back long from his imprisonment in Beirut. Unfortunately we couldn't stop to hear him but it was a lovely experience.

Chapter 40

David's boss decided to have a rare holiday with his wife and left detailed instructions for Dave during his absence, mainly concerning Rosie the house cow. Rosie was collected from her field a quarter of a mile away, each evening, led along the road to the farm where she was milked by hand, then settled into the paddock behind the house with hay and cow cake to munch on. In the morning she had to be milked again before the return journey to her field. Dave pursued this regime for a couple of days before attempting to streamline the operation. He found his old bike and began cycling along the road, leading Rosie back with her halter in his hand. By the end of the fortnight, he felt that he had really achieved something in time and motion study and couldn't wait to tell his boss.

"Do you know, I've managed to get Rosie milked and the milk into the 'fridge in ten minutes?"

"Well done Dave, that's marvellous," congratulated the boss with a grin. Dave couldn't believe it when a fortnight later he met the boss on foot accompanied by Rosie, udder swinging pendulously, as she followed him docilely along the road.

"Why are you walking Rosie along the road after all my hard work with her?"

"Um," replied the boss, "I'm walking her along the road to be milked at the farm, because... I like to walk her back in the morning!"

Dave, for once in his lifetime was speechless.

Dave's boss was unique. He had a real affinity with chalk. Not sticks of chalk but great hunks of it. I noticed a chalk mark on the side of a barn that said 'switch' I followed it round a corner and eventually came to an electric switch where another notice also read 'switch'! The grain dryer had been installed twenty years earlier but the words, 'Caution, vehicle likely to veer across the road,' could still be seen chalked on the end of it, which had been written when it was towed along the road.

David discovered him walking round the farm buildings with a hen tucked under his arm.

"Mr. Trewby, why are you carrying a chicken around?"

"Well, I'm trying to put all the chickens together in a run. I had some more in a sack which I put down while I caught this one but I've forgotten where I left it."

There was a wide variety of poultry on the farm besides the chickens. There was a flock of Muscovy ducks that had the habit of flying at a height of about three feet from the yard, across the road to the stream. Andrew made a notice, "Caution, low flying ducks!"

There were also geese, bantams and 'phantams', which are a cross between pheasants and a bantams.

Mr. Trewby was wearing a panama hat one day with a cap on top of it. The answer to the inevitable question was that his daughter had just given him his cap which he had left at her house and he didn't want to lose it.

Auction sales were the breath of life to him. The first week that Dave was employed by him Mr. Trewby took him to a sale at Cambridge. We heard that he arrived home once with a vintage basket work bath chair – he thought it would do to push his mother around. She understandably wasn't keen on the idea. However, a use was found for it as it was just right for blocking a hole in the fence through which the sheep were escaping.

Dave was rushing around one day and was stopped in his tracks by Mr. Trewby,

"Dave, just watch that hen, she's trying to find somewhere to lay her eggs." It was a lesson Dave never forgot and we make a point of sharing these moments with others – it may be a rainbow or a bird gathering building materials for a nest but they seem nicer for being shared.

A notable character who was involved with the farm was Bob, a 'retired' gamekeeper. He was eighty when we first met him and had been living in a retirement home when he was 'rescued' by the boss who employed him to cope with the vermin on the farm. He trapped moles, caught foxes, and shot magpies. All around the farm tracks could be seen the results of his labours strung up to warn others of their fate. He had travelled widely in the Merchant Navy during the war and had an endless store of stories about his exploits. Our teenage boys loved to listen to him and learnt a lot about life in the Navy from him. He lived in a small cottage by himself – plus various chickens, ducks – and Gertie, the pig. The livestock, including Gertie, were allowed the free run of the house and Bob regarded them as his family. The boss's wife was visiting Bob one day and seeing Gertie very much at home in front of the fire, remarked, "Gertie shouldn't be in here Bob, what about the smell?"

"Smell? She don't mind it!"

Dave had an urgent call from Bob. "Dave, Gertie's down the old well and I can't get her up." Dave went to have a look, and sure enough, ten feet down a hole, which had been covered with an old piece of wood, was Gertie. He fetched a tractor and some rope, climbed down the hole, and with great difficulty managed to get Gertie secured fore and aft. He then had to climb out of the hole and fasten the other end of the rope to the fore loader of the tractor. With Bob steadying Gertie and shouting instructions, he slowly raised the fore loader and Gertie with it, until she was clear of the hole. It was a very noisy operation as Gertie complained bitterly the whole time but soon stopped when re-united with Bob who took her away for a feed to help her get over her ordeal.

Neither Bob nor Gertie learnt however and a few months later quite early in the morning I answered the door to a frantic knocking.

"Mrs. Sullivan where's Dave? Gertie's disappeared."

Just then, the 'phone rang,

"Do you know if Bob's lost his pig?" it was our local bobby.

I managed to locate Dave and he picked up Bob and they drove to where Gertie had been seen – the council estate at the other end of the village! There, surrounded by disbelieving residents, some in dressing gowns and curlers, was Gertie, munching away at the green grass of the children's' playground. They managed to bundle her, protesting vociferously, into the back of the van. Later they learnt that a car driver at 5.30a.m. had had the experience of nearly colliding with Gertie on his way to work along the main road.

Bob was always busy and kept the local fox population down, earning pin money at the same time by sending the skins to a furrier in London. He was greatly missed on the farm when he finally had to retire and move into a more convenient dwelling.

Chapter 41

Dave decided to buy a pig and breed from her so that we'd have our own supply of pork, also providing something in the way of sex education. We had reared a pig once before when the boys were younger and it proved to be a huge success with no problems when it came to transforming pig into pork. Peter would lean over the fence of the sty and scratch Polly's back, murmuring, "Just look at that lovely crackling!"

Pinky, the sow was introduced to a borrowed boar and after the correct length of time went into labour. That particular evening, Dave had to visit the boys' school as sex education was about to appear on the curriculum and parents were invited to view the proposed course! The boys had come home with a lot of homework so I ended up acting as midwife to the pig. I was assured that pigs had no problems giving birth; all I had to do was to ensure that she didn't lay on them, and move them under the infra-red lamp as they arrived. The first five arrived with no trouble and then everything seemed to stop. I went indoors, hoping that one of the boys would like to join me as it looked as if I was going to be out in the shed for some time. They had finished their homework but were now watching "Blake's Seven," one of their favourite programmes.

I returned, alone, to the shed. Pinky was sleeping while the piglets milled around squealing. Nothing seemed to be happening but I couldn't leave them so fetched a book to read. Dave was convinced that Pinky would have at least ten piglets, and after another half an hour, I felt I needed advice. I went back indoors and picked up the 'phone.

"Hallo Alan, I need your advice about a farrowing pig."

"I'd be pleased to help but surely Dave knows what to expect?"

"Yes, he does, but he's gone to a sex education meeting at the school."

Alan laughed. "What do you want to know Eileen?"

"Well, Pinky's had five piglets and nothing has happened for nearly an hour. Do you think she'll have any more?"

"It's quite likely, give her a bit longer, but if you're still worried in half an hour, I'll come round and investigate."

I expressed my thanks and hurried back to the maternity ward. Thank goodness, another two piglets had made an appearance and another one popped out as I watched. She went on to have a total of eleven although Dave had to destroy one as it was badly deformed.

"Had a quiet evening dear?" queried David when he came in.

"I bet I learnt a lot more about sex than you did," I retorted.

Chapter 42

Susie, Andrew's goat was expecting a happy event any day. She missed the village green but Andrew discovered that she enjoyed the grass along by the river so tethered her there. When he brought her in one evening she seemed rather restless and went into labour. She still hadn't given birth before we went to bed but Dave promised that he'd get up at 5am to check her. She was still straining so Dave investigated and found that one kid was presenting wrongly. He endeavoured, to turn it but unfortunately a hoof caught the wall of the birth canal. He managed to extricate the two kids, both dead, but realized that Susie was in a bad way. He 'phoned the vet. and was able to take her straight into Andover to the surgery. There was nothing the vet could do except supply antibiotics. She lived another two days before she died. We all shed tears as she had become a real part of the family.

We thought that a meal out might cheer us up and give us something else to think about. We decided to go to a restaurant that we had enjoyed before and found it just as good as before – with no cooking or washing up! The waiter presented the bill. Dave fumbled in his pocket and pulled out a £10 note.

"Have you any money with you Eileen?"

I had forgotten to put my purse into my handbag. The boys had no money either and it was pre-credit card days. We looked at each other and Dave eventually called the waiter over and explained our dilemma.

"If I leave my watch as security, could I return tomorrow and pay the balance please?"

The waiter went to confer with the manager who agreed that it would be all right. Dave collected his watch the next day but we were shy of returning to that restaurant again.

Another member of the family was Toby, Andrew's ferret. He was very tame and each evening would come into the kitchen and enjoy a plate of cat food with Joey, the cat. He lived in the shed in an escape proof metal cage and was fed on dead day old chicks that I had to fetch every so often from the local chicken processing factory. Andrew divided them up into tubs, each sufficient to last a week. These then went into the freezer for Andrew to take out at the beginning of each week so Toby could have fresh food every day. Sometimes he'd be taken out for a walk in his little harness and proved a source of great interest to everyone. One evening when everyone was out except me, I had a 'phone call from the farmer to say that he had just seen a ferret disappearing under the granary, which was on staddle stones. Sure enough, Toby's cage was empty; I went over to the granary and luckily met the farmer's daughter on the way. By lying down we could see under the building and as Toby was a yellow ferret, we could just see him. Penny went round the other end of the granary while I banged my end. She managed to catch him by dropping a large flower pot over him and then sliding a piece of wood underneath it. I insisted after that, that Andrew fitted a padlock to Toby's cage.

Chapter 43

A year after David had been to the Antipodes, Andrew was able to follow in his footsteps and do part of his pre-college experience in New Zealand as he was going to Seale Hayne Agricultural College to study for HND in Agriculture. A friend decided to go with him, working on a different farm not too far away. It was vastly different to Ibthorpe, and Andrew spent a lot of time learning about trees, lopping off lower branches. There was also a large flock of sheep on the farm, Andrew and another employee shared a house and the cooking, he soon began to appreciate mutton- it was the only meat they had! The two boys spent Christmas with Nigel and Marion where David had been the previous year. They even managed a swim in the sea on Christmas Day. Andrew and

Debbie, the oldest girl (there were five daughters altogether plus one son) had grown up together until they were eight years old so it was interesting for them to meet again, ten years later. Andrew and Steve enjoyed their time in New Zealand and bought an old car to tour South Island, picking up hitchhikers and camping out at night. They returned to the U.K. via Los Angeles where they stayed for three weeks, another unforgettable experience. They managed a trip to Disneyland but as the arrangements they had made to stay with friends while in the U.S. fell through, found themselves quite broke. They discovered however that T.V. studios were glad of an audience and spent whole days watching different episodes of films being made. They also found out that doughnuts in Los Angeles were cheap and filling! The last night they were there they stayed in a four star hotel, courtesy of the airline, as the flight was delayed for twenty four hours so were able to make use of the swimming pool. It was good to have Andrew home again; he worked on a farm locally for a few months before going to Devon to obtain his HND.

Peter's interests were somewhat different. He was musical, playing the piano and also the tuba! He was remembered at school for covering his tuba with fairy lights and playing a piece called 'Tuba Smarties' in a school concert. He went to Surrey University where he gained a degree in Electrical and Electronic Engineering. Both boys married farmers' daughters within a few months of completing their education, Andrew and Rosemarie have a boy and a girl while Peter and Brenda have two boys and a girl.

10. Going it alone

Chapter 44

In 1985 David decided to take the big step of becoming self employed, starting a share farming enterprise, he supplied the shepherding skills while others supplied the sheep for the project. This posed a big problem of where to live as we had always occupied tied cottages and hadn't earned enough to save up for a mortgage. We wanted to remain in the area and affordable houses were in very short supply.

We managed to rent a property in another village about four miles away but we knew it was only a temporary arrangement. The few months that we were there was a sharp learning curve for David. He had no real base from which to work and it took time to locate suitable fields in which to graze the sheep. The first area to become available was the steep fields around Inkpen Beacon; they had not been grazed for years and were full of ragwort, brambles, thistles and other weeds. Today the downs are clean and the sheep still graze there. There were other areas available and gradually David was able to use them. Most of the fields had inadequate fencing for keeping sheep so David had to get that sorted out first. This was made possible owing to the invention of a portable electric fencing product that was able to work with sheep.

Harry Ridley, a farm manager living at Chilbolton near Andover had pioneered the system and Dave acted as a guinea pig in trying it out. Basically it consists of three strands of electric fencing with insulated fence posts that just have to be pushed into the ground at intervals. One end of the wires is connected to a portable battery powered energizer, if the sheep touch the fence they receive a sharp electric shock and soon learn to avoid it. It revolutionized sheep keeping which was ideal because the nature of Dave's job meant that the sheep were continually changing their pasture. He was able to use cow paddocks in the winter when the cattle were brought into sheds and also water meadows that were unsuitable for anything else except grass. He devised a system of payment for the pasture he used calculated on the number of sheep that were utilizing the grass per day.

We heard that owing to the death of the occupant, there was a small cottage empty in the lane where we had been living. We were able to view the property before it was officially on the market. It was in an ideal situation but very small with just one bedroom and a landing upstairs, two rooms, kitchen and bathroom downstairs. Although the boys were away at college and university, they were home quite a lot and still needed a base. We talked it over and decided that if we could extend at the back and make a proper room out of the landing, we could manage. It was a grade two listed building so planning permission had to be obtained which eventually was granted six months later. Unfortunately we didn't have the resources to do the building work for another year so we managed with the minimum of alterations plus a caravan parked behind the house. When the work was finally finished it was a great day and although even now it's still a small house, it's warm and cosy and we love it. Now there's only the two of us we have plenty of room and situated as we are in a quiet lane overlooking fields, the situation is idyllic.

Some of the share farmers owned land so a scheme had to be worked out for them as to the method of payment. It was quite a complicated method of sheep keeping as the grazing was very scattered. The furthest that sheep could walk was about four miles a day, so if there was a longer move, Dave had to arrange an overnight stop for them. Other local farmers were quite happy for Dave to fence a small section of a field for his sheep to have 'bed and breakfast. He tried to move them on early in the morning with as little disruption to traffic as possible. It's not practical to move sheep on foot any more as the traffic has increased so much

Some years later when the stewardship scheme came in and S.S.S.I's (Special Sites of Scientific Interest) were introduced there was a demand for sheep to graze these areas so the price Dave paid for grazing was reduced.

Lambing was difficult that first year as there seemed to be only one small field available about four miles from where we were living, which would be suitable for the job. He only had a flock of about three hundred and would be able to move them on once they had lambed. Another difficulty was that we had no caravan in which to keep all the equipment needed and warm up any cold lambs – and shepherds. We did have an Ifor Williams horse box which would have to suffice; it was far from ideal as there were gaps in the sides and no means of heating. The weather was atrocious, wet and windy, and the field quickly became a quagmire. We had to manage without any outside help and although I'm no good at helping ewes in trouble, I could help with feeding any weak lambs and moving the sheep that had lambed into another field. Dave read of a farm auction not far away, one of the items was a caravan so he decided to go to it.

'The Colonel' was able to come to assist me, he loved helping and was more able than I was to manage ewes in difficulties. We looked around the sheep together at regular intervals. It was towards the end of lambing so things were fairly quiet; I noticed a ewe in trouble so we went to have a look. The colonel strode across the field. I followed him feeling like the page in 'Good King Wenceslas' walking in his masters' steps! He dealt with the problem and as we squelched back to the horsebox I asked him,

"Colonel, what made you take up keeping sheep?"

He thought for a moment.

"Well Eileen, when people retire – especially from the services – they don't like being idle. Some take up golf or bowls or angling. Some like messing about in boats, but I like sheep".

He owned twenty-five ewes of his own as there were a couple of acres of land by his house. He borrowed one of Dave's rams each year watched his flock carefully so he could calculate just when the lambs were due and was always proud to announce his 175% lambing rate. He owned a couple of sheepdogs, Flanders of whom more is written elsewhere and Rosie, a rather odd looking smaller one. He wore a dog whistle continually around his neck and revelled in his standing as a sheep farmer.

I had a 'phone call one day to say that there were two stray dogs in a field where we had a few sheep. This particular village was about ten miles away and I had no idea where Dave was. I went looking in some of the places that he might be but couldn't find him so I decided to go and investigate. I wished that I hadn't! If only mobile 'phones had been invented then. I located the field and discovered to my horror a German Shepherd dog and a Jack Russell had the sheep pinned against a fence. Every time one moved the dogs attacked it. Some of the sheep had torn flesh and they were all absolutely petrified – so was I! I found a telephone box and dialled 999, I explained the situation to the police who said that they'd send somebody to deal with it, I couldn't bear to watch the sheep so went back home.

Dave arrived at the scene a couple of hours later at the same time as the police. The dogs had gone but they had left a scene of carnage behind. A couple of the sheep were dying, Dave had to destroy another three ewes and five of the others were badly injured. He had an idea whose dogs they were as he had seen them earlier in the village. When the policeman and Dave went to the house, the owner declared that the dogs had been in their kennel all afternoon, but when asked to get them it was discovered that the Jack Russell had some blood on it. However, the police were unable to charge the owner as it couldn't be proved definitely that they had been the dogs in question.

Chapter 45

Sheep were purchased as ewe lambs when they were weaned, usually in September, kept for a year and then sold for breeding, they were then known as 'shearlings'. This system worked well for a few years but then the bottom fell out of the shearling ewe trade which meant that Dave was left with five hundred breeding ewes. He had no choice but to breed from them himself as there was still a good market for lambs.

Eighteen years on we own six hundred and fifty ewes although at one time we had nine hundred. David also has sheep on an agistment arrangement with three farmers which provides a steady income. A further alteration took place when the price of lambs dropped so after a lot of thought and prayer, Dave took a big step and changed to lambing in May. He reasoned that by keeping the ewes on grass he could save money on feeding costs as by the time the ewes were heavy in lamb, there would be plenty of grass available. The system works well and many others have followed in his footsteps although he seems to be the only one keeping sheep outside all the year round.

Sparsholt Agricultural College asked David if he would teach practical shepherding skills to the lowland sheep course that was in operation. This was just for one day each week plus a week of intensive shearing tuition in the spring. The students were also allocated an 'adoptive farm' where they spent one day each fortnight in a 'hands on' situation. The alternate week Dave taught them the various practical skills they would need when they left Sparsholt. It was a financial proposition and guaranteed a regular income which we badly needed. Dave thoroughly enjoyed introducing many youngsters to the joys of shepherding and many of the students went on into the sheep industry.

The week spent shearing with the students was very hectic for us all as I had to supply lunches and snacks for the sixteen students plus others who turned up. Normally, he only had half the students at a time but they all came as it was easier to get all the sheep shorn in the same week. Dave usually had six shearing machines working and the students took turns at shearing, wool tying and keeping the pens filled. Many of the girls found shearing very hard work – which it is – but some of the boys went on to become expert shearers and have taken part in competitions. Occasionally the student would have an accident and sheep were nicked with the cutter or in some cases quite badly injured but they had a lot of expert tuition that week which they wouldn't have received otherwise. We were able to have the use of a neighbouring farmers' barn as often the weather would be unsuitable for shearing but it had to be done on that particular week. He was able to get his sheep shorn for nothing in payment. The students spent a couple of weeks on their adopted farms at lambing time, gaining valuable experience which would be difficult to obtain in any other way.

This course along with many others is no longer available at Sparsholt as the emphasis is on rural pursuits rather than 'real' farming. There are now equestrian, fishing, green-keeping and game-keeping courses amongst others.

We eventually had our extension built which provided us with a large kitchen/dining room complete with Rayburn – essential for warming new born lambs and drying out wet clothes. Both boys brought their girl friends home although not usually at the same time. Brenda was at Surrey University with Peter, she was a farmer's daughter from Cumbria and Rosemarie had moved into the area and was working as a veterinary nurse. Her home was in Devon and her father was also a farmer so both girls were quite at home.

Having sheep scattered over three counties, Hampshire, Berkshire and Wiltshire in up to a dozen locations at any one time, produced logistical problems moving the sheep around. Dave decided to make a sheep transporter to tow behind a tractor. He bought a Scammell semi-trailer and, with the help of the local blacksmith, designed a double-decker, sheep-carrying unit. The bottom deck had a slatted floor, there was a ramp to load the sheep on to the top deck and the sides were constructed from galvanized iron. Each deck was divided into three compartments and the total carrying capacity was about one hundred and twenty ewes, depending how much wool they had on them. It was a wonderful piece of equipment and made the job much easier. It was Highly Commended in a Farmers Weekly innovation competition and won a prize in the Newbury Show, Eventually a tarpaulin had to be made to cover the top to comply with E.E.C. regulations. Unfortunately it had a very ignominious end......

The owner of the house advanced along the drive, rifle in one hand, mug of coffee in the other and a bottle of whiskey under his arm!

"I thought these might be helpful."

The double decked sheep trailer with one hundred sheep on board had just demolished his hedge, causing chaos and killing seventeen of them. David wasn't sure which the property owner wanted him to use first – and for what purpose. He was too busy trying to rescue the sheep which was proving to be difficult and dangerous as the trailer was on its side. It had been loaded unevenly and as Dave negotiated a tricky double bend in the road, the sheep slipped to one side and altered the centre of gravity. Some sheep managed to escape and disappeared up the lane while others had to be pulled out. Eventually the trailer was empty and Dave had to use the rifle to dispatch some of the animals that were beyond help. A neighbouring farmer arrived with his four wheel drive tractor and righted the trailer, while Dave, having summoned help in the form of his shepherdess, rounded up the runaways.

Unfortunately, the trailer was beyond repair but the insurance money paid for a Mark two version of the trailer. This was a cattle lorry body which already had two decks. Once again the blacksmiths expertise was sought to make a drawbar and construct inner compartments. This version had very efficient air brakes and is still in use today.

Accidents did happen although thankfully very rarely.

"Eileen, now don't worry, but David is on his way to Swindon hospital in an ambulance!"

A neighbour had been walking on the Downs near Inkpen Beacon and noticed Dave knocking in fence posts with a two handed post banger. He started knocking in another one and as he lifted it up for another swing, to her horror he hit his head! He was knocked out and as the accident took place over the Wiltshire border he had been taken to Swindon, thirty miles away. I hastily packed pyjamas, slippers and shaving gear and drove to the hospital. He was kept in for a couple of days and enjoyed the enforced rest, suffering no ill effects – or so he said!

Chapter 46

Another problem was sheep that knew the grass was greener the other side of the fence when often there was no grass there.

"Mrs. Sullivan I've just returned from walking the dog and met a sheep in the footpath leading to the water meadows. I managed to move it back towards the gate, but it could get out on to the road."

I jumped into the car and drove the half-mile to the end of the footpath in the middle of the village. I was only just in time as the ewe was heading for the busy main road. I manoeuvred it back the way it had come, not easy without a dog, and discovered the lady who had 'phoned and her husband also trying to catch the ewe. With the three of us on the job, it should have been an easy matter, but nothing is ever simple when sheep are involved. Unfortunately, the gate through which it had to go was of the 'kissing' variety so it couldn't see where it had to go. The man tried holding the gate open but the sheep baulked, turning tail and headed for the main road again. I managed, with difficulty to head her off but she broke through a hedge into a garden.

Then the inevitable happened, the ewe made a dash for freedom and as she could run considerably faster than me, she reached the main road first. I wasn't far behind her and by frantically waving my arms, I managed to stop the traffic. A motorist leapt out of his car and joined me as the sheep hurtled the two hundred yards to the corner of the road and turned along it. I rounded the corner just in time to see her disappearing into the drive of a house. I left my new found assistant guarding her while I used the phone in the nearby home of a friend to try to contact David. I tried on and off for the next three hours but discovered later that his mobile phone was on his motor bike – he was in the Land Rover! The ewe, meanwhile, had progressed to the back garden of the house where the owner, an elderly lady, was sitting enjoying the sun, accompanied by her carer.

The carer was fascinated by the unexpected visitor.

"Och, the puir wee thing can bide here in the garden. Would it like a drink?"

Leaving the exhausted ewe receiving a lot of tender loving care, I enjoyed a welcome cup of tea with my friend before going home to await Dave's return.

When he walked through the door, starving hungry, I rushed him straight back out, telling him my tale of woe as we went. In my haste, I tripped over a paving stone and landed heavily on the ground. No bones were broken but my dignity was hurt. We found the ewe grazing peacefully on the lawn still being admired by her new friends. She gave herself up with only a token struggle, but we never did discover how a heavy woolly sheep could negotiate a kissing gate.

Chapter 47

Dave used to sell his lambs to the local abattoir six miles away which was very handy as he could load them onto his big trailer and take them with the tractor. We could also take any casualty ewes – any that might have a broken leg or similar and we could get there in quarter of an hour. One afternoon, Dave came in about half past three.

"Eileen, could you take a large lamb to the abattoir as its broken its leg and although I set it, it won't mend. Ask them if we can have it back as meat. The abattoir closes at four o'clock so you'll have to go straight away."

"How am I going to get it there?"

"I'll put it in the boot. I can prop it open a bit, it can't get out so you'll be all right."

I went out to the car. Dave loaded the animal, Pip decided to come with me so he went in the back seat. I reached the main road and turned right to go up the hill. Just as I was passing the pub, I heard a noise, and looked in my mirror. To my horror, I realized that the boot had opened and the lamb was standing in the road looking very bewildered. I stopped the car, ran back to the lamb and wondered what to do next. Just then a young couple came out of the pub, and stopped in surprise at the scene that greeted them.

"Please could you help me? I think I'd better put the lamb in the car."

"What do you want us to do?" they asked.

"If we can get her to the car and open the back door, she could lay down on the floor."

We somehow got the lamb to the car but as I opened the door and Pip saw what was coming in, he jumped up on to the parcel shelf. He wouldn't move so I left him there and reached the abattoir just in time.

We can no longer take casualty sheep there to be slaughtered as it had to close for killing when the new E.E.C. regulations began. Their abattoir is now situated in Wales after being briefly located at Funtley. The carcasses however, are sent to our local abattoir for butchering which seems a lot of unnecessary movement. Dave now sells his lambs to a cattle dealer who lives in the village and they travel to an abattoir near Yeovil.

If we need any lamb we either buy a whole carcase at the local abattoir, or if Dave has any hoggetts to get rid of he takes them to an abattoir at Devizes. They will kill and joint them, and bag them up ready for the freezer. Dave's brother-in-law will exchange half a pig which he rears in his garden for a lamb so we usually have more than one killed at a time. Another farmer friend had arranged to pick some up for Dave and arrived one day with five carcasses and brought the two which were for us indoors.

"Could you use all the offal?" he queried, "nobody else wants it".

"Yes, we're fond of liver and I have a good recipe for stuffed hearts."

I surveyed the gory heap before me. I'd have to go and buy some bags as I only had small ones. All I could buy at the local shop was one size – big. Armed with a sharp knife and chopping board I advanced upon the offal. I hadn't realized that the liver was still attached to the hearts and lungs. I plunged my knife into the first 'pluck' to detach the heart. It parted company with the rest of the offal quite easily. I hate handling lungs; they resemble huge pink lumps of rubber. Still it had to be done so I sliced the tissue joining the liver and lungs and put the heart in a bowl with the liver. The dogs would enjoy the lungs for their suppers. I now had the task of slicing all the liver, a very messy, slippery job; just then, the doorbell rang.

"Excuse me, does Captain Fairfax live here? I have a delivery of oil for him."

"Captain Fairfax is dead," I replied with my carving knife still in my hand and my apron covered in blood. The driver's face blanched and he took a step backwards.

"Mrs. Fairfax lives round the corner, third cottage on the left."

He mumbled a hasty thank you and jumped into his lorry. I wondered what I had said to provoke his reaction!

I returned to the kitchen to resume my gory job. I bagged and labelled the liver, it would last us for quite a long time. I looked at the hearts and lungs and had an idea...

Haggis! Why not? I found my Mrs. Beeton (Delia didn't deal with regional dishes in her book that I owned) the recipe was understandably in the Scottish section with cock-a-leekie and clapshot.

I went outside to pick some herbs, rosemary, parsley, I couldn't seem to grow basil but I knew that a neighbour had some. Oatmeal, onions, suet, salt, pepper? I had them all. Whiskey? I thought there was some in the cupboard that David had been given when he was talking to a sheep group meeting in Kelso three years ago. He only used it if he had a cold so there was still plenty of Glenfiddich left. I found my largest saucepan but thought I'd start with two plucks. I heaved the lump of pink rubbery lungs towards me.....

I never did make the haggis. I didn't have the stomach for it!

At one time we had to cut the carcasses up ourselves. Dave bought a surgical saw and butchers knife from a local disposal firm where everything imaginable can be found. We'd sometimes end up late in the evening chopping up the meat which I would have collected in the car earlier in the day. Dave was invariably tired and often missed the chopping board – the kitchen table still bears the evidence!

In 1987 Dave had to take an enforced rest when he discovered that he had a hernia, quite common in farmers I'm afraid. He had never had an operation, before so it was a new experience for him although he would only be in Winchester Hospital for two nights. When the anaesthetist came for a preop talk, Dave opted to have an epidural as the recovery time was quicker.

The surgeon began the operation and after a while asked conversationally,

"What work do you do?"

"I'm a sheep farmer in the north of the county, near Andover."

"That's interesting. Have you been doing it for long?"

"Yes, nearly thirty years and if you do this job properly, I hope to go on for another thirty."

The surgeon stopped what he was doing, "You're joking of course?"

"No, I love my work."

"I can't wait to retire."

"Well! This is a fine time to tell me."

Dave went on to make a full recovery but often wondered when the surgeon did retire.

Chapter 48

"Is that Mr. Sullivan? I've had your name given to me by the N.F.U. as possibly being able to supply some Scotch Blackface sheep for use in a film."

"Yes, I'm David Sullivan but I haven't any Scotch Blackface, my sheep are mainly North Country Mules. I have an acquaintance who does keep them, how many did you want?"

"I'd like about twenty in August if it's possible."

I'll find out for you. Could I have your name and telephone number and I'll ring you back. By the way, what film is it?"

"My name is Rona Brown and I specialize in finding animals for films. The film is 'Mary Reilly', it's a new version of the Dr. Jekyll and Mr. Hyde story starring Julia Roberts and John Malkovitch."

This sounded exciting and having inquired what she was prepared to pay for the hire of the sheep, Dave contacted his friend – and ascertained that he was willing to supply the sheep when needed.

"Hello Rona, the sheep can be available on that date. Where do you want them taken?"

"Good. Can you bring them to the Isle of Dogs by 7 a.m. on August 28th? Could you also supply a pen for them? You can be in the film as an extra if you like; you'll be paid for that of course in addition to the hire fee, any helpers that you need to bring could join you.

'This gets better and better,' thought Dave.

"I shall have to bring my son to drive the Land Rover with the fencing for the pens, and extra help. Is that all right?"

The night before the trip I had a house full: Andrew, our shepherdess, plus a friend who was travelling with Andrew. They loaded Andrew's trailer overnight with the fences plus hay and water troughs for the sheep to use and collected the sheep, putting them in a nearby field until the morning.

They set off at 4.00.a.m. thinking that three hours for travelling would be ample. I had worked their route through London with the aid of a borrowed A-Z.

At 8.a.m. the 'phone rang, "Where are the sheep?"

As we didn't have a mobile phone I couldn't be of any help.

The call was repeated an hour later. I was beginning to get worried, I would have been even more so if I had realised what was happening…

The convoy had made good time up to the M25 but then the traffic became heavier and Dave's speed dropped right down. As they approached Central London it came to a standstill. Dave and Andrew had managed to stay together and were now in the middle lane of a triple carriageway, crawling along in bottom gear. Then the unthinkable happened. The engine of

Dave's Land Rover overheated and he came to a full stop. With a cacophony of horns blasting away around him, Dave lifted the bonnet – and decided to remove it altogether to keep the engine cool – tying it on the roof of the Land Rover. They drove for a bit further like that but ground to a halt again. There was no way a breakdown truck could reach them even if they had summoned one.

Dave ran back to Andrew's trailer and pulled off a bale of hay, "Have you got any string there Andrew?"

"Yes, here's some, what are you doing?"

Dave tied the hay at the back of the horsebox and shouted to Andrew, "Push!"

Andrew dutifully drove closer to the horsebox behind Dave's Land Rover and pushed. With a shudder the box and vehicle began to move to the relief of the many exasperated drivers around them. After a time, Dave was able to restart the Land Rover and continue independently of Andrew. Eventually they found the film set, quite a difficult job as the A-Z from which I had planned the route was out of date and a lot of roads were now one way streets! A large warehouse had been turned into an 1800s Glaswegian abattoir. They found Rona who was virtually tearing her hair out with frustration, unloaded the sheep into a hastily erected pen and were hustled into a trailer to be made up.

It was fascinating. Exactly as seen on television with lighted mirrors, plush chairs and make up personnel hovering .Dave had a make up cape whisked around his neck, mutton chop whiskers added and make up that gave him a swarthy appearance.

"Now for your hands," the glamorous young lady cooed.

She picked one up – and nearly dropped it.

"Tracey, have a look at these. They're more like dinner plates! Right colour too, they won't need making up."

"They're genuine shepherd's hands," stated Dave proudly, "They're that colour because I didn't have time to wash them when I arrived and I've been unloading sheep!"

The hands were hastily dropped and Dave was sent on to 'wardrobe' where he was pounced upon by a young man.

"Hallo, darling. Now you need gaiters, a shepherd's smock and a hat." Before Dave could get his breath he was kitted out and sent to rejoin the others who were attired in a similar mixture of garments.

They were shown the inside of the 'abattoir'. There were pens with cattle in either side of a central passageway and further along were 'carcasses' hanging up constructed of plastic and looking very realistic. Great vats simmered in the background sending up clouds of steam, making the atmosphere very dim and eerie. They were briefed about the sheep and their own roles and had to wait outside until their moment on stage arrived.

Dave had to drive the sheep along the aisle followed by Mr. Hyde who was shadowed at a distance by Mary Reilly, his maidservant. Andrew and the others had to busy themselves helping with the sheep or, in the case of Louise, walking along with a basket over her arm. It took about three takes to get the scene right but after that, they were able to watch what followed.

They were fascinated when one scene called for a bullock to be pole axed. This was achieved by an animal trainer teaching the animal to fall at a given signal when the axe dropped.

They all enjoyed a three course meal eaten in a restaurant trailer, along with the stars of the film and altogether really enjoyed their glimpse of stardom. The day wasn't over however. They decided to wait until after the rush hour to begin their journey home so left London about 6.30.p.m. It was a lot easier going home and all went well until they were nearly at the Newbury turning from the M.4. Dave ran out of fuel! By this time it was dark and raining and neither Dave nor Andrew had brought any spare fuel not realising the stop/start journey they had had on the way there would drink the fuel so rapidly. It was decided that Andrew would tow David as there wasn't much traffic. All was fine for half a mile and then a car with a flashing blue light passed them and signalled for them to stop.

"Are you aware, sir that you're breaking the law by towing in this manner?"

"Well officer there didn't seem to be any alternative and as you can hear, there's twenty sheep in the trailer that need to get home as soon as possible."

"We'll let you off this time as you're nearly at the turning and after all, we would have had to send for a tow truck."

Half an hour later, they were home, as glad to be back as I was to see them. They discovered later that there had been a rail strike that day, hence the volume of traffic.

Mary Reilly has never been on the cinema as it was panned by the critics although it is available on video but we have never seen it.

Chapter 49

Travelling around the countryside, Dave often saw things that were quite unique. As he went through one village, a tractor pulling a trailer came out of a side road and set off along the road in front of him. Nothing unusual about that, there were always tractors around. They didn't usually have a 1950's juke box on board though! Dave realised that it must have come from the village hall as it was the only building along that lane and he knew it was being renovated. He followed the tractor; he had no choice really as the road they were on was quite narrow. After about a mile, the road began to go up a hill. It was very steep as it was part of the down land south of Hungerford. Dave suddenly realised that the juke box wasn't secured in the trailer – and the tailgate wasn't fastened. Still the tractor was only travelling slowly but gradually as the tractor climbed the hill, the juke box began trundling backwards along the floor of the trailer. Dave sounded his horn and flashed his lights but the only reaction was to make the other tractor speed up.

The end was inevitable. Dave slowed up so that he wouldn't be hit by the falling juke box. It hit the road with a crash and burst open scattering records everywhere. Dave stopped his tractor and went forward to survey the damage. The other driver was oblivious at first to the events happening behind him but, glancing in his mirror, he realised that something wasn't quite right.

He climbed off his tractor looked back down the hill and up at the trailer in disbelief. He joined Dave in contemplation of the wreckage.

"My juke box!" he wailed, "I've only just bought it. Paid £100 for it."

"Whatever were you going to do with it?"

"I bought it as an investment; I thought I could hire it out to pubs and things. Do you think I'd be able to mend it?"

Dave stirred the debris with his foot and picked up a record. "Not without a lot of this," he grinned handing him "Help" by the Beatles.

Driving home Dave remembered a disaster that he had once with a tractor when he was cutting grass for silage. They were a man short and he put some thought into how he could save time.....

He set off across the field with the forage harvester hitched on behind – and a barrel of treacle, which was usually added to the grass at a later stage of production, propped up on the tractor mudguard. He turned the tap on the barrel open slightly and glanced behind to make sure the treacle was trickling out sufficiently. Yes, it looked fine; perhaps the barrel could be a little higher. That was better it would spread more evenly like that. The trailer was nearly full of grass when the tractor hit a concealed rock! The treacle barrel shot into the air followed closely by a treacle- covered Dave. That was the last time that he tried to cut corners.

"What's the matter with you?" Dave asked, getting out of the Land Rover. He had just driven into a field where he had about three hundred ewes and their young lambs. The ewe he was asking continued to run around looking very distressed with a lamb close at her heels. "Where's your other baby?" Dave looked around and could see no lamb by itself and knew that the ewes in this field all had twins. There was a river running through the field and the ewe was running up and down the bank. Dave looked in the river, no sign of a lamb, perhaps it had fallen in and been swept away as the water was flowing quite fast.

As he stood there, he heard a faint "Baa"– which seemed to come from beneath his feet. He lay down on the river bank and saw that a pipe discharged into the river just above the water level. The ewe came charging along, stopping when she reached Dave and bleated loudly. The answering "Baa" came from the pipe! There was only one thing to be done. Dave stripped off – at least the sun was shining – and lowered himself into the chilly water. He peered up the pipe, and could just see the lamb. He reached in and could feel a little woolly tail, but as he grabbed at it the lamb moved further up the pipe. There was a trickle of water coming from it but Dave discovered that it was just wide enough for him to wriggle into. He couldn't even crawl but had to slither along somehow.

He could only hear the lamb now as his body blocked out the light – and it was moving further away. Dave tried reaching out in the darkness but the elusive animal retreated even further. Dave stopped moving and thought!

Nobody knew where he was and if he couldn't get out himself, someone would find a heap of clothes with a pair of boots on top, a Land Rover and the two dogs. There must be another way of doing it. Perhaps if he found the other end of the pipe he could flush the lamb out. No, that wouldn't work as it would get washed out into the river and get swept away. He decided to get out of the pipe and reconsider. Painfully he wriggled backwards, grazing his knees on the way, he was glad to get out and bathe his wounds in the river. He regained the bank, dried himself somehow on his vest, pulled on his jeans, and then had another idea. He fetched the crook from the Land Rover and with difficulty caught the ewe. One handed he managed to remove his jeans and lowered himself and the ewe into the water. Holding the ewe up awkwardly to the pipe entrance, he tried to make her bleat. She wasn't co-operative. So he imitated her probable bleat into the pipe and from a long way away came a pathetic answering "Baa". The ewe heard and began calling frantically for her baby. Dave could hear it now scrabbling along the pipe. At last it was nearly there so he heaved the ewe on to the bank getting drenched in the process, – there's nothing wetter than a wet sheep. He grabbed the lamb and reached above his head to deposit it on the bank. The ewe whickered in delight and sniffed the lamb all over to ensure that it was hers, then calling to her other lamb, trotted off with them both.

Dave dried himself for the second time and dressed. He checked round the rest of the ewes and continued on his rounds. He returned to the field some hours later to make sure everything was in order. Leaving the field, he had to pass the farm manager's house and his wife, Diane came out to meet Dave.

"Been swimming again Dave?" she queried.

Dave laughed, "How did you know I'd been in the river?"

"I saw you"

"You couldn't have done, I was at least a quarter of a mile away."

"I had a pair of binoculars and went up into the bedroom!"

Chapter 50

Not everything that happened had a humorous side though. Dave had moved some sheep one day but had to leave two behind in the field as they were clearly unwell. The next day he was about to return to the field to treat them and remove them to his 'hospital', when he had a phone call to say that some sheep had escaped from the field five miles away to which he had moved them, and were heading for the A34! It took him a couple of hours to get them back where they belonged and mend the hole in the fence through which they had escaped.

He drove to the field that the sheep had vacated the previous day, accompanied by Kate, our part time shepherdess. As they went across the field he could see that one of the sheep was dead but wasn't surprised as she was old. He put her into the trailer and then he and Kate had to chase the other ewe, which although sick, was still quite lively. Dave managed eventually to catch her and loaded her into the trailer as well. He secured her with a special restraint which kept her lying down safely. They drove across the field to the dead pit which was in the corner, unlocked the padlock which secured the lid, and dropped the dead sheep in. As they went towards the gate, two gentlemen stepped out from behind the hedge.

"Where are you taking that ewe?"

"I'm taking it to my 'hospital' field so that I can treat it and continue to look after it. Who are you?"

"We're from the Trading Standards Office and have been contacted by the R.S.P.C.A. who received a 'phone call to say that there was a dead sheep in this field. Are they your sheep?"

"Yes, they are, and I intended dealing with them earlier but had an emergency elsewhere."

"Well, you can't transport that animal in that trailer, it's not suitable for the job and I see you have fencing stakes in it and what is that device around its neck?"

"That is a Gambrel restrainer and is approved for use by the Sheep Veterinary Association. The sheep is lying quite comfortably and in my opinion there's nothing wrong with the way that it's being moved."

"Would you please remove it from the trailer?"

David lifted the ewe out and put her on the ground where she lay secure with the restrainer round her front feet and behind her neck.

"We've sent for the Ministry vet. who will be here shortly. It's also an offence to transport a live sheep in the same trailer as a dead one."

Just then, another Land Rover drove into the field and Andrew climbed out.

"Everything all right Dad? I was passing and saw these men peering through the hedge."

"Yes, it's O.K. they're from Trading Standards and are concerned that I'm breaking the law in moving this ewe."

"What's wrong with it?"

"Here's the vet now," one of the men stated, we'll see what he has to say."

They explained the story to the vet. who turned to Dave, "What, in your opinion is wrong with the sheep?"

"I think the ewe has pneumonia, she's old and I was taking her to my 'hospital' field for treatment but was prevented from doing so. She's in urgent need now and I'm not sure whether she will live, see what you think."

The vet knelt down and examined the ewe, "Yes, I think you are right but I don't think she will recover even with treatment. It might be best to put her down."

"That's what I think too." Dave went over to his Land Rover and came back with his skinning knife in its sheath. He bent over the ewe.

"What are you doing?" shouted one of the men.

"I'm going to put her down"

"You can't do it with a knife, it's against the law."

"What am I supposed to do then?"

"Well, you must use a humane killer or else shoot it."

"I haven't either and this way is quick and painless as I learnt to do it the right way in New Zealand and can break its neck simultaneously with cutting its throat."

"You can't do it."

Dave turned to the vet. "As you're here, please could you do it with your humane killer?"

The vet looked a bit sheepish, "I haven't got it with me."

One of the other men butted in, "Where is the place that you were taking it to. Can we go and see it now please?"

"I ought to deal with this poor ewe first. She's been lying here for an hour and is deteriorating rapidly."

"You can deal with her afterwards but I want to get this business sorted out," replied the official.

There was nothing that Dave could do except drive the mile to his 'hospital' field where the officers examined the other sheep he had there and wanted to know their histories. They took various photographs of Dave's trailer, the ewe, the restrainer and drove away after telling Dave they would be back to examine his whole flock.

David went to see a neighbour who had a rifle and went to the field with him, where they dispatched the ewe.

Soon after, Dave received a communication from Trading Standards stating that they were bringing charges against him. There were four separate charges. Using an unsuitable trailer to transport a sick ewe, mistreating it when he took it from the trailer, using a device to restrain it that could cause suffering, and carrying a live and dead sheep in the same trailer!

He sought advice from the solicitor recommended by the N.F.U. and we began to try and source every available help. We managed to find the leading sheep vet in the country who had introduced the restrainer from New Zealand, and he offered to appear for us when the case came to court. One of the charges wasn't valid as a particular E.E.C. case number was quoted which had since changed. The other two charges although were rather ridiculous, the solicitor felt he would be able to cope with.

A year after the incident, Dave had to appear at the local magistrates' court in front of three magistrates. He had several witnesses to testify as to his working methods, ability and character, as well as the sheep vet. Andrew and Kate were cross- examined, also the farmer who eventually shot the sheep. Proceedings were halted for lunch and it amused me to see Dave and one of the officers having quite a conversation after lunch.

The court resumed and soon the magistrates retired to consider their verdict. The atmosphere was very tense, especially when one of the magistrates requested clarification on one point from the clerk of the court. He read from a book, all I heard was, "If found guilty, the sentence is £300 fine or six months in prison." I went outside and stayed out until Dave came out beaming.

"Cleared of all charges and awarded costs," he said, "Come on, let's go home"

That wasn't the last we heard from Trading Standards however. A couple of years later Dave came home from work feeling unwell with a temperature and couldn't eat his food. I had to go out that evening and after fetching a pillow and his sleeping bag he settled down in front of the fire. He was woken up by the doorbell and groggily went to the door.

"Mr. Sullivan, we've had a report of a sick ram left out in the field and we'd like to see it please." It was the same Trading Standards officer that had visited him before plus a vet. that Dave learnt later had been summoned from Reading!

"I know I have a sick ram, I think he has pneumonia, I've given him oxytetracyclin and will treat him again in the morning."

"We want to see him now please."

Dave found his coat, boots and a torch, at least the ram was only in the meadow opposite the house but he felt so ill. They walked across the field together, it was a clear frosty night but Dave didn't feel much like a walk. As they went in the direction where Dave knew the ram to be, they could see an odd shape ahead.

"Whatever is that?" queried the officer.

All was revealed when they neared the unusual lump when a head appeared from under a duvet- not the rams but a woman's; she was under it with the ram!

"I was trying to keep it warm," she stated.

"Let me have a look at it," the vet said.

The woman started "cooing" to the ram and generally getting in the way.

"Please go home to your husband and take your duvet with you," requested Dave and reluctantly she went off.

The vet ascertained that it was pneumonia and that Dave had administered the correct treatment.

"Could you put it in a shed somewhere?" the Trading Standards officer asked.

"It's a lovely night," said Dave, "it would be better out here" – (pneumonia does respond better in fresh air). "What you're asking is for me to put it out of sight."

"Well, yes, I am."

The men went off and Dave fetched a wheelbarrow, somehow heaved the ram into it, and pushed it up to the barn. He returned home just before I did and was still shivering when he went to bed.

Some of the land that we use for grazing has the Test Way passing through. This long distance footpath stretches from Totton near Southampton to Inkpen Beacon, a distance of over seventy miles. At weekends and holiday times it becomes quite busy with ramblers. Some walk a certain distance each day and then find Bed & Breakfast accommodation before resuming their journey. As a result of this traffic we get a lot of queries about the sheep. The sheep also have the annoying habit of lying down on the footpath to die – in spite of having a large field to choose a more private place. Sheep also get on their backs and lie there with all four legs in the air, as, when they are heavy in wool, their centre of gravity changes. If they are not righted they can die as the gases produced from the grass they have eaten build up inside them.

"Are you the shepherd's wife?" I answer the door yet again to a hiker in walking boots, woollen socks, pullover and woolly hat.

"Yes, I am. What's the problem?"

"I've just walked through the meadow opposite and a sheep doesn't look well. I don't really know anything about them though; could you come and see it?"

I accompany the hiker; halfway along the path is a ewe, on its back. I stand behind it, put my hands on its backbone and with a gentle lift I push the sheep past its centre of balance. It scrabbles to its feet and without a backward look runs off.

Chapter 51

David couldn't manage his job without his "tools of the trade" – his sheepdogs, usually two, although he really preferred to have three, so that if one was unwell or had been working extra hard, he could rest it. At present we have two, Pip who is six, and Woll, aged two. They are both unusual looking dogs for border collies as Pip has a heavy curly coat, more like a poodle's and Woll is smooth haired. If Pip was a cat, he'd only have seven lives left as he's had a couple of near fatalities.

David was making hay one day in a nearby field and Pip was running behind him most of the time. Dave suddenly missed him so stopped the tractor and whistled for him. No dog appeared. Dave climbed off his tractor and set off to search for him. He whistled again. This time he could hear a noise coming from a clump of trees, it was a splashing sound. Dave broke into a run; he suddenly remembered what was in the middle of the trees, – a disused concrete tank that had been a reservoir. He climbed over the barbed wire fence and looked down into the murky water. "Pip! How am I going to get you out of there?" The water was about six feet below the top of the tank and there, swimming (doggy paddle of course) was Pip, very tired and with no way out. Dave ran back to the tractor and fetched his metal shepherds crook and returned to the poor dog. He lay on the ground at the edge of the tank and stretched out the crook towards the exhausted dog, as it swam past. After several attempts he managed to hook the crook beneath Pips collar. A wet dog is almost as heavy as a wet sheep but with a tremendous effort Dave managed to haul Pip up the sheer side of the tank and grab hold of his collar. Pip was relieved to be on dry ground and had a vigorous shake, making Dave nearly as wet as himself. The pair of them had to lie down in the sun for a while to dry off.

The other near death experience he had was when he was with Dave on another farm. David had been dosing sheep with a drench and having finished the job, went to put the rest of the chemical away in the lockable shed. He was busy sorting things out and suddenly became aware that Pip was rooting around under the bench.

"Come out Pip," and he yanked on his collar to remove him. It was too late however as some slug bait was open and Pip had decided to try it! By the time he had found out where the nearest vet was located, the dog had already started fitting. The vet (whose surgery was at Alresford), pumped out his stomach and then sedated him, telling Dave to 'phone in the morning. He was kept sedated for three days before the vet decided to bring him round. I had the job of 'phoning to find out whether I could fetch him or…

He was all right and very pleased to get home again.

Other dogs we've had weren't so fortunate. Laddie was one of the best dogs we've ever had, very gentle and marvellous with children and yet a superb sheep dog. He was five years old and in his prime, we were going on holiday the next day so there was a lot of work to do. Dave had used him to move ewes and lambs all day, it was quite warm but cloudy. As

Laddie brought the last lot into the field he suddenly collapsed, panting badly.

"Quick Kate help me to put him into the trough, I think he's got heatstroke." Dave shouted.

"Do you think you ought to Dave, it could give him a heart attack?"

Dave stopped just before he dropped him into the trough.

Kate had worked for a vet once and knew more about that sort of thing than he did.

"Perhaps you're right; I'll get him to the vet."

The vet took him outside and played the hose over him, "The best thing to do in a case like this is to cool him down as soon as possible."

It was too late though and dear Laddie died.

Another dog that came to an untimely end was one of Jack and Jill's offspring, Bob. He was the only one we kept of the litter and was a beautifully marked dog, a tri-colour. He was with Dave one day when I received an urgent 'phone call to say that there were three sheep on the road. I managed to reach Dave on his mobile and thankfully he wasn't too far away and said that he'd deal with the problem.

The doorbell rang. "Eileen could you meet David at the Methodist Chapel, The dog has met with an accident and Dave wants you to take the car down as he thinks that the dog will have to go to the vet."

I reached for the car keys and drove the few hundred yards to the chapel. Dave was kneeling on the ground cradling Bobby. "I think he's broken his back, can you put the back seat down?" He managed to climb in with the dog and I drove as fast as was safe into Andover to the vet. The vet came out to the car and confirmed Dave's diagnosis. He went back into the surgery and returned with a syringe in his hand. It was all over.

"The sheep went behind the Chapel," explained Dave, "so I sent Bob in to get them out but they turned right instead of left. A Range Rover came round the bend, missed the sheep but couldn't avoid the dog."

Jake was another really good dog, a tricolour and very good natured. He had one problem however; he tended to have an epileptic fit every few months, usually soon after being let out in the morning. The vet was consulted but expressed the opinion that as he was such a good dog and the fits were so infrequent, it would be better not to give him medication, as it would slow him down. He was a good worker and along with Jill and Jimmy made a good team. Dave came home one evening, however with a very sad looking dog that couldn't put his back leg down. He had run out in front of the Land Rover, Dave couldn't miss him and caught him a glancing blow. It was back to the vet.

"He's dislocated his hip," stated the vet, "I'll strap it up and he must rest it. Bring him back in a fortnight."

I had him indoors as he couldn't jump into his kennel and took him out for short walks. He quite enjoyed his life as a house dog but I was looking forward to taking him back to the vet where, hopefully, he would get the all clear. It wasn't to be though.

"Strapping it up wasn't the best idea I'm afraid, his hip is still out of joint. I won't strap it up again but make sure he doesn't use it.

Eventually, he did recover although he tended to get more tired. Three years later, he began to limp again. Back to the vet. "He's developed arthritis in that leg I'll give you some medication." It was like a new lease of life at first but then his fits started to increase in frequency.

"It's probably the medication, it'll settle down."

It didn't and once again I had a house dog but one who became increasingly distressed. The fits caused him to twitch violently, and he lost control of his bowels and bladder. It seemed to upset him so much and when he began having several fits per day, David decided that the kindest thing was to have him put down.

The intelligence of the dogs never ceases to amaze us. Dave went to check the sheep one day soon after lambing and discovered one ewe only had one lamb instead of two. He hunted all round the field, behind all the bushes but couldn't find it. Jimmy, our current dog at that time, decided to go rabbitting.

"Come here Jim, you're supposed to be helping me find a lamb."

He wouldn't come but continued to dig.

"Come here," Dave shouted.

In desperation he went over to the dog, which was still digging in a rabbit hole. Dave pulled him away and then had an idea. He lay down and felt down the hole.

"There's nothing there, you silly dog."

He continued to grope around and then felt a piece of string. He pulled it gently until he could reach the end, to discover that it was attached to a lamb, its tail, and eased it out of the hole.

"Sorry Jimmy, you're a good dog."

The ewe sniffed the lamb carefully and once she was sure that it was hers, let it have a welcome drink and moved away up the field.

Bobby was the only dog we ever owned that was home bred and we've had very few registered dogs. Most of them are bred by local shepherds or farmers and Dave has been able to see the parents working so has a good idea of the dog's potential. They don't come into the house as they're often muddy or wet and as they have to work outside in all weathers, it's not good for them to get too hot. They have good kennels, raised above the ground with a sleeping area containing plenty of straw, and a living space with a slatted floor surrounded by wire netting. During the day the kennels are propped open and one of the tame sheep learnt that there was often left over dog food to be had. She'd get on to her hind legs and somehow pull the dish out – not that there was ever many leftovers. The dogs used to be fed with a biscuit mix and tinned food, but now that there are new dry mix foods with all the necessary nutrients, they have that. They just have one feed a day at night as then they have plenty of time to digest it. The ducks have learnt that if they wait beneath the kennels, sometimes some scraps might fall through the slats for them. The dogs resent them and as they eat, keep up a constant low growling, to which the ducks are oblivious. Dave has a seven month old puppy now which still needs three meals each day so has scraps at one feed, bread or biscuits with an egg or milk at another, and puppy biscuits at night. Bud, the puppy has just started his training with sheep, going out for half an hour each day with Dave and a few sheep. After a couple of weeks he's already beginning to respond to various commands and appears to have the potential as a good sheep dog. He is also helping to move sheep when it's an easy move, and then Woll has to stay in the Land Rover as he has bad habits with sheep which Dave doesn't want Bud to learn.

Chapter 52

Dave rarely has to call the vet as the vet we've had until recently, always maintained that Dave knew more about sheep than he did. Unfortunately, he has decided to specialise in domestic animals so we've had to transfer to a vets' practice in

Salisbury, twenty- five miles away. Dave had a problem with a ewe just before lambing one year. A ewe seemed reluctant to get to her feet and seemed to be in pain. He couldn't think what the problem was so took her into the vet who diagnosed a dislocated pelvis.

"Can you treat her?"

"Well, I can't do it until tomorrow morning. She'll have to have an anaesthetic and will probably lose the lamb".

Dave took the ewe home. He was fairly sure that she was expecting twins and the vet's bill would be quite a lot. Then he had an idea…..

An hour later, he had the ewe on the front lawn. It was dark by now so he switched on the outside light just as a car pulled up at the gate.

"Hallo Dave, is this the patient?"

"Yes Chris, the vet thinks it's a dislocated pelvis, what do you think".

Chris ran his hands carefully over the ewe,

"He's right. I've never done this before but I'm willing to have a try. Just hold her in this position can you?"

Dave positioned the ewe as requested and after a few minutes work there was a definite 'click'.

"That seems to have done it, let's see if she'll stand up."

They carefully lifted her on to her feet. She stood; wobbling for a few minutes and then gingerly took a couple of steps.

"Thank you so much Chris, how much do I owe you?"

"Nothing, Dave, you've been a good customer of mine, let's call it one for the memoirs."

The osteopath stepped into his car and drove the mile up the lane to the thatched cottage where he lived.

"It's David Sullivan here, please could you cancel the appointment with the vet?"

"Why, has the ewe died?"

"No, it's very much alive; the osteopath sorted it out for me".

A fortnight later, the ewe produced two healthy lambs.

One of my favourite lambs was George – born on St. George's Day. He was soon joined by a ewe lamb that had to be called Mabel. We had a spare dog kennel at the time where they were able to live so we could shut them in at night. George was a most unusual lamb. Most lambs utter a "Maa" as soon as anyone appears with a bottle. George wasn't content with that and bleated "Mumm". I went out one morning to give them both their breakfast. Mabel came running to meet me but there was no sign of George.

"George, where are you? Do you want some breakfast?"

"Mumm," came the muffled reply but where was he? I called again and located him; he was under an old caravan! I knelt down and peered underneath. He was completely wedged under the axle; there was no way I could get him out without help. I located Dave via his mobile 'phone and he quickly came to George's rescue.

Chapter 53

David often received invitations to speak at various functions around the country ranging from W.I. meetings to prestige dinners. Sometimes I was able to accompany him.

One such invitation came from "Teagasc," the Irish equivalent of MAFF. Would David like to take part in three meetings for Irish farmers where he would be the third speaker each time? They had heard of his lambing methods and felt he would be interesting to follow the other two speakers. One was from the Irish Government and her aim was to persuade the Irish farmers to ear tag the sheep to comply with E.E.C. regulations. The other speaker was from

Teagasc, he was dealing with sheep costings. David was really there to provide light relief. We had never been to Southern Ireland and the organizers were happy for me to accompany David. The three meetings were in Castle Bellingham, Port Laoise, and Enniscorthy, the first two actually being held in the hotels in which we would be staying. We were asked if there was anything that we would like to see while we were in the Emerald Isle, perhaps we'd like to see the sights of Dublin?

What Dave really wanted to see, was a genuine Irish farm so that was arranged. We packed our wellies and coats in a rucksack; put some tidy clothes in a suitcase as we would be eating in hotel dining rooms and travelled up to Heathrow. We parked the car in a car park about a mile from the airport and caught the courtesy bus. It was quite a walk to our departure gate but we were soon on board and flying above the clouds. Just before we landed, the captain made the usual speech, thanking us for travelling with Aer Lingus and please would we fasten our safety belts. He then added a postscript,

"Would anyone who has been on a farm within the last two weeks, report to immigration please?"

Dave dutifully found the right building which was apparently deserted.

"Anyone there?" he called. From a back room, came a man polishing his glasses.

"Can I help you sir?"

"Yes, I've come to report the fact that I work on a farm."

The man scratched his head and looked puzzled.

"Why should I want to know that?"

"I don't know," answered Dave, "the captain said we had to report here if we had been on a farm."

Light dawned and the man disappeared into the back room again, returning with a spray pump.

"Lift up your foot so I can see the bottom of it."

Dave felt like a horse about to be shod as he obeyed the instructions.

Two squirts of the spray on the sole of each shoe and he was declared disinfected enough to walk on Irish soil.

Meanwhile, I was in the baggage hall waiting for our case to appear. A cat in a basket came round on the carousel. Gradually all the cases were claimed but there was no sign of ours. The cat in the basket came round again, and again, and again! Dave had rejoined me so went to find someone to ask about our case. The cat came round again. Nobody else was waiting but the carousel continued to perform its endless round. Dave returned.

"Have you got the tickets?"

"I thought you had them". I hunted through my handbag while Dave searched his pockets.

"Would Mr. Sullivan please report to the Aer Lingus desk?"

Dave went off again but realised he would have to go through the departure gate and not be able to return. (The cat was still sitting patiently in its basket going round on the carousel).

I waited by the gate. Dave returned. He had met the man from Teasag and also discovered that our case was on its way back to Heathrow. He also found out that we had dropped our tickets – at Heathrow! We arranged to collect them at Dublin airport on our return and Aer Lingus would deliver our case when it arrived on the next flight from Heathrow, to the hotel where we were staying at Castle Bellingham.

We were treated to a welcome cup of tea in the airport restaurant by Mr. Scully, our host, and then driven the forty miles to the hotel. The only luggage we had with us was Dave's rucksack with our wellies and coats!

The hotel was very nice, set in beautiful grounds, large bedrooms and downstairs in the lounge a big log fire. There was about two hours before dinner so we hoped our case would appear before then. Dave had a sleep and we found some magazines to read. The speaker from the Irish Government appeared so Dave was able to chat with her. The Sound Engineer arrived, he was hard to understand as he was very Irish, and his name was Mike! A couple of other people from Teagasc turned up but still no case. We moved into the bar with everyone and were served with pre-prandial drinks. Then, when we had almost given up hope of seeing our case again, the porter brought it in.

Dave and I have always been able to get changed very quickly but we broke the record that evening.

After dinner it was soon time for the meeting. About two hundred Irish farmers crowded into the Function room. Dave set up the viewing screen and arranged his slides; they had been in the suitcase too. The three speakers and the chairman were fitted with radio microphones and the equipment tested. (With the sound engineers name being Mike, Dave thought it gave a whole new meaning to being 'miked up!')

There was a lot of discussion over the proposals suggested by the lady from the Irish Government after which Mr. Scully from Teagasc spoke about costings.

Dave's slides and talk were well received as everyone was rather disturbed by the proposals from the Irish Government and needed something they could relate to.

This was the pattern at the other two gatherings where about the same number of farmers were present. It was rather like a 'road show', with all the speakers, the chairman and Mike staying at the same hotels with us.

We were taken to a farm where a visit had been arranged, which at first looked very imposing but only part of the house was in use. We enjoyed a meal of real Irish stew that had been cooking in the Aga while Dave was taken on a tour of part of the farm. The owner wasn't actually Irish but had emigrated from England. We discovered that at one time he had worked on the same farm in Kent where we started our married life. After lunch we toured the rest of the farm – we were glad we brought our wellies and coats as it was cold and windy.

One hotel we stayed in was at Port Laoise quite near a big prison. We had the morning free so had a wander around the town. Dave, as usual, was fascinated by butchers' shops and there were items there we had never seen before. We had seen black pudding, (although I'd never eaten it) but not white pudding. The last place we stayed was Ennicorthy and to get to our room we had to pass through the bar where an Irish 'wake' was taking place – quite an experience.

We reached England without further mishap but would like to return one day to Ireland and see a bit more of the country.

Dave also had a couple of visits to Scotland. I went with him on one of them and as it was in February, by the time we reached the borders, snow was falling. We stayed with some acquaintances in Peebles and the next day, Dave went on a farm walk with the other members of a May lambing group before speaking to them after lunch. I just joined them for lunch and the talk having spent the morning in a warehouse of a wool company. A few weeks later he was asked to go to Kelso, but decided to go by train.

Chapter 54

The Foot and Mouth outbreak in 2001 affected us although we had no cases of the disease, but there was an outbreak in a cattle herd two miles away from one of our flocks. We had various flocks on stubble turnips over an area of about twenty miles and nothing could be moved. Hay had to be taken to the sheep which necessitated a lot of travelling and physical hard work. Eventually some of the sheep had to be sent for slaughter on welfare grounds which was upsetting. When the restrictions were partially lifted, we were able to move a flock to set aside land across a lane from the field in which the lambs had been wallowing in mud. This, of course, needed a movement licence which had to be obtained from Salisbury Trading Standards office as the field was in Wiltshire. The vet had to be present and disinfected straw laid on the road, but the effort was worth it just to get the sheep on to dry ground.

Lambing was another major problem as the system we used, needed the lambs and their mothers to be moved on to clean pasture the day after the ewes had lambed. We always moved them before lambing to the lambing field where we erected pens and had a good system of moving them from a day area to a night area. They were on the Downs which was the most exposed area that we grazed as it faced north and even though we didn't lamb until May, the weather wasn't very good. The motor bike was very useful and Dave devised various aids to help him. The elastrator rings were threaded on to a big split pin shaped like legs at one end to stop the rings falling off, which fitted on to his belt. He used a back pack for other essential lambing aids such as iodine for spraying the lambs navels and aerosol paint for marking them. He was unable to move the ewes and lambs to clean or sheltered pasture so animals died that under normal conditions he would have been able to save. Because the downland where the ewes were covered a very large area, it was difficult to catch any ewes in trouble so they mainly had to manage by themselves. If lambs hadn't sucked he was unable to catch the ewes and couldn't then grab the lamb to help or bottle feed it. He was also unable to have any outside help as anyone who could have helped him, had sheep elsewhere to be cared for. Understandably, we had a lower lambing percentage than usual and more ewe deaths but it wasn't as bad as Dave had feared. In May when the restrictions were lifted subject to extensive licensing and he was able to start selling the lambs from the previous year, the price had dropped dramatically from £48 per animal in February down to £18.

One thing however that helped to lighten the general air of despondency was the hatching of ten ducklings in the hedge opposite our house. We knew one of our semi-wild Muscovy ducks had been sitting there; she used to waddle over the lane to the garden every day for water. It was impossible to see her, followed by her ten babies, crossing the lane, and not smile and she brought a lot of pleasure to everybody. Eventually, they all took up residence in the garden and became quite tame, even waddling indoors to find me if they wanted food. The water bowl was only an old washing up bowl but it had to double up as a bath when they thought they needed one and three of them could squash into it together. We tried to persuade them that the chalk stream at the end of the lane would be a more suitable home but within twenty-four hours of herding them into the water meadow, they were back.

When we went to France for our annual holiday we dutifully reported our farming connection when we landed at Ouistreham as requested, but apart from a very cursory glance into the car boot by the gendarme, there was no real search. We had been informed that under no circumstances were we to take foodstuff into France. The owners of the gite in which we were staying were English, and were renovating a neighbouring barn for use as a house. When they had arrived at the port, their caravan was completely stripped and searched for any foodstuff.

When we are in France, we always try and visit the nearest sheep market and that year there was one taking place about ten miles from where we were staying. We went along and as usual, were amazed at the differences between British standards and French ones. Most of the sheep arrived in small quantities, no more than twenty, and some came in the back of Citroen vans and we even saw one ewe in the boot of a car – secured by chains. They were herded into pens with the sellers standing by, either ready to extol their virtues or guard them from being stolen! Most of the sheep were poor specimens, some with defects that would never have been allowed in to an English market. The system of selling is totally different too. At an appointed time a bell was rung and warehouse-coated buyers appeared clutching what looked like a book of raffle tickets. The buyers descended on the pens and business was conducted at a furious rate with the buyer offering the seller a ticket on which a figure had been scribbled. The seller invariably tore the ticket up, throwing the pieces in the air with an emphatic "Non!"

The buyer would move on to the next pen, climbing in to feel the sheep and repeating the offer to the seller. After an incredibly short space of time, the transactions were completed and lorries arrived to load the sheep for transport elsewhere. Some sheep had obviously been hand reared as farmers' wives took a sad "Adieu" to their charges. Electric prods were used and the whole business seemed totally alien to us. Sheepdogs were carried in cages under the lorries between the back and front wheels.

We kept a low profile as we felt that with the foot and mouth crisis in England, our presence might not be appreciated.

We visited a theme park one year near Poitiers devoted to sheep! The French have a real flair for making museums and exhibitions interesting and this one was no exception. The grounds were divided into small enclosures each containing a different breed of sheep which came from various countries. The housing in the enclosures reflected the country of origin. The sheep from Russia had a very ornate building with cupolas on top, no mistaking where they were from. Somali sheep had a typical grass roofed mud hut. Commentary was provided by 'Walkman' type cassette players with the translation that was requested. We found this quite amusing as it was in the form of a conversation between a grandfather and grandson explaining what the different sheep were and the main function of each of them. The commentary about Britain was particularly funny as one lot of sheep on display were Black Welsh Mountain. So....."Grandfather, why are those sheep black?"

"Well Nicholas, in Britain everyone wears black clothes so black sheep are needed".

There was also a small pack of wolves in an enclosure surrounded by water which seemed odd in a 'Parc des Moutons'.

No sheep flocks in France seemed very big, about the most we saw in one field was fifty but on the whole, there was usually only a dozen. One year we had the privilege of spending a night on a farm with a family we had befriended the previous year. The farmyard was surrounded by enclosures containing, rabbits, chickens, ducks, turkeys, geese, and guinea fowl. The kitchen garden was about half an acre in size absolutely full of beans, carrots, peas, onions, leeks and other vegetables with which I was unfamiliar. Jean-Luc's daughter Isabel was at university in Paris and every fortnight a consignment of farm food would be sent or taken there as it was requested as part payment for her board and lodging at the place where she was staying. Jean-Luc and his wife Claudette spoke no English and our French is quite limited. Ludovic, their son was learning English at school so we were able to make ourselves understood. They invited another English couple who lived in the next village to dinner that evening which was a memorable occasion. The other couple were both artists, earlier we had been to see an exhibition of their work which was arranged in a converted cow shed. Unfortunately, David and I have no idea about art but managed not to say anything that would be misconstrued. The outstanding attribute of the French we discovered, was their politeness to each other. Any transaction was accompanied by a handshake – even buying a gas cylinder at a garage – and I was treated to a kiss by Ludovic in the morning when I had breakfast. Teenagers greeted each other similarly in a very natural manner.

On one of our trips to France, we spent a day with another Nuffield Scholar Jean-Marc whom Dave had met at a Nuffield Conference. He and his wife Jeannette rented their farm but were having quite a struggle. Jeannette ran a small catering business and Jean-Marc had employment as a translator in a Bubble Gum factory owned by an Englishman. They were renovating a couple of farm cottages to use for a Bed and Breakfast business and asked us if we'd see if the rooms needed anything suitable for the British trade. I suggested a hospitality tray as it's something I think is lacking in French holiday accommodation. We had a lengthy meal with them and a couple of Polish men who were working at the factory. There was a different wine with every course which Jean-Marc produced from a big trunk in the corner of the room, I kept to water. I had taken a tin of custard powder with me as I knew it was hard to obtain in France. I ended up having to make it!

Chapter 55

It is unwise for pregnant women to work with sheep as there are various diseases that are transmissible to humans and some that could cause abortion. It's very difficult when working with sheep to always observe strict hygiene rules as hot water is unobtainable out in the fields. Plastic gloves are a help and also 'wet wipes'. Dipping sheep is a hazardous job too as the chemicals used are very toxic and yet until recently, just how dangerous they were wasn't really understood. I can remember one dipping when the weather was very hot. The Sparsholt student who was helping stood on an 'island' in the middle of the swim round circular dip, wearing only a pair of shorts (it was a boy) and flip flops. The trouble is that sheep need dipping in the summer and protective clothing is very hot and restricting; it consists of an all-in-one waterproof suit, rubber gloves, a rubber apron and a face mask! It is also important for anyone working with sheep to be vaccinated against tetanus as the micro-organism can easily enter through a cut.

Parties of schoolchildren often come to see the sheep at lambing time. However well Dave tidies up before they come, inevitably they will discover a dead lamb somewhere which holds more fascination than all the live ones. Some children are fascinated if a birth occurs while they are there, others are repelled! Dave had to assist with a birth one day while a party of children hung over the side of the pen.

"I think there's something wrong with this lamb." David warned.

There was, it was dead. There were a few "Aahs" but the one thing they all wanted to know was, "Is it a boy or a girl?"

David usually gives them a demonstration of rubber ringing a lamb's tail and the bolder children will have a ring put on one of their fingers to feel what it like. Some lucky ones will go home with a 'balloon' – a blown up long plastic glove! We always make sure that there's warm water and soap for the children to wash their hands. A few days later, a 'thank you' card usually arrives from the school made by the children complete with pictures of the lambing field. We feel that their imaginations have been stirred especially when one had a picture of Dave and Kate holding hands!

Chapter 56

David decided to buy another sheepdog as Pip is getting rather old and slow and Woll isn't always reliable. As it takes at least eighteen months to train a dog, Dave started enquiring amongst his shepherd friends to discover if there were any puppies around. One shepherd's bitch had just produced five pups, two of which were dogs which David preferred. When the puppy was eight weeks old, it could be weaned from its mother. We had our youngest grandchild, Michael, who was six with us when Dave went to fetch it so he accompanied David on this important errand. Dave had decided to call the puppy 'Bud' as it seemed to suit him so after a lot of fuss from everyone, especially Michael, Bud became part of the family. I always have to look after a puppy until it has had all its vaccinations although it has its own kennel outside. Dave feels it is important that each dog has a place that belongs just to it although Pip and Buddy decided to exchange kennels after a few months! We had found a 'traditional' kennel for Bud but he liked jumping up into Pips and as Pip isn't as good at jumping as he was, they swapped. Buddy was a very biddable puppy and soon learnt the basic commands although could be easily distracted. When he had finished his injections and could walk along the road, I taught him to sit whenever a vehicle passed and he was soon doing it without being told.

As time passed, he was able to go out with the 'big' boys. He rode in the front of the Land Rover in the passenger seat as Woll tended to bully him. He became very enthusiastic about sheep and as soon as he was released from the vehicle, would find the nearest flock to 'eyeball'. In the back paddock as there were no sheep, he used the long suffering chickens – Pip preferred the ducks! As he has grown older, he tries the same tactics on a horse that lives in a nearby field.

Buddy is now a year old and has benefited from a month away in the Brecon Beacons with a friend who is an expert 'dog man'. We were going on holiday for a fortnight and as Kate would have the other two dogs plus Poppy, her own bitch, Dave felt it would be easier to board Buddy out. The dog returned, having had expert tuition and Dave had some valuable advice as to his future training. John advised him to start using a special dog whistle – the same sort that 'the Colonel' used, it had to be worn around the neck on a cord as there was a real danger of swallowing it. It was quite small and was gripped with the teeth. As Dave was using the motor bike more, he discovered that it was impossible to put his fingers in his mouth to direct the dogs.

Woll is a strong dog in every way; Dave uses him more for pen work as the sheep take notice of him. He can jump incredibly high and clears a five barred gate with ease. He had a nasty experience a few weeks ago.

Dave, Woll and a colleague, Ted, went to count the sheep in a particular field. It was an impossible job to do so they decided to put them in a pen. Dave left Ted erecting the pen just inside the field gate while he and Woll walked to the other end of the field where the sheep were. It was an awkward shaped field, long and narrow with a bend. The other dogs were out of the way in the Land Rover.

Dave walked along the side of the field in case there were any sheep in the bushes. He sent Woll to go behind the flock of around three hundred to start moving them. After scouring the hedges for stragglers they began the long drive back to the pen. The sheep were moving nicely, when suddenly, the sheep simultaneously did a 'belly flop' and tried to pull their heads and legs underneath them. Dave stared in amazement. He had never seen that behaviour in sheep before during the forty-seven years that he had been shepherding. Woll, who was close behind the sheep, yelped and ran off at great speed into the distance. Dave carried on walking towards the sheep when he became aware of an army of flying insects in yellow and black striped football shirts! Wasps! He began to run – a real achievement as he hadn't been able to do so for some time. The wasps were keeping up with him and attacking any bare flesh that they could find the back of his neck and his hands seemed particularly attractive to them so he tried to pull his jersey over his head. Unfortunately, some must have been trapped in it so they started on his head and hands.

"Ted, get in the Land Rover and drive out of the field before you get attacked." Dave shouted as he neared the pen, "I'll shut the gate."

Ted looked up from the job he was doing in alarm, and seeing the sight of Dave running, dropped his tools, and jumped in the Land Rover. Dave closed the gate and joined Ted in the cab.

"Stop while I call Woll."

Dave gave a piercing whistle and Woll came running up, soaking wet from his immersion in a water trough where he had taken refuge and with his usual mighty leap, cleared the gate and allowed himself be hauled into the Land Rover.

Dave and Ted returned to the field later in the week to find no sign of the wasps and successfully counted the sheep. Anti-histamine tablets and cream are now part of the first aid kit but hopefully they won't be needed again this summer.

Chapter 57

One problem that has arisen recently is the disposal of dead stock. Although every effort is made to keep sheep alive, inevitably there are deaths among the three thousand sheep in Dave's care. Years ago it was an easy matter to dispose of them. A 'phone call to the local hunt would ensure that any carcase would be collected within twenty-four hours – end of problem. The meat was fed to the hounds, the bones went for bone meal and there was a market for sheepskins so the huntsmen were repaid for picking up the dead stock.

Another alternative was the local knacker who operated about five miles away. He would accept carcasses; the meat was stripped from the bones, cooked, and went for dog or cat meat.

In the eighties, the BSE crisis arose and there was no market for bone meal. The hunts had more carcasses than they needed so would only collect from farms over which they hunted.

The on farm burial pit was introduced to deal with the problem. These were usually dug with a JCB digger, had to be sited well away from any possible contamination to a watercourse and away from access by the public.

When David returned from his visit to the Antipodes, he came back with another idea of how to deal with dead sheep!

In Australia, cull sheep were slaughtered, skinned and, cooked outside over open fires in forty gallon drums. When the meat was cooked, the bones were hooked out, barley meal was added and the resulting mixture stirred with a post hole borer. It was then tipped into 12" deep trays, left to solidify and cut into 12 cubes with a spade. Theses were then frozen and each dog received a cube every day for its supper.

Dave decided to try it, with a couple of carcases, lit his fire, cooked the meat, fished out the bones, solidified the mixture and fed it to the dogs...

They refused to eat it!

An idea that *did* work, however, was a 'slink pit'. This works because the carcasses are broken down by bacterial action quite quickly and was approved by MAFF. Dave had a seventeen-foot hole dug and sank an empty 500-gallon tank into it after removing the base. A three-foot pipe led to the surface, which he sealed with a lockable manhole cover for complete safety. Dead animals were dropped into the tank to decompose. However, after two years of use the volume of dead animals overtook decomposition, so another solution had to be found.

Dave set fire to the top layer, and this – surprisingly – worked, so he decided to turn the whole thing into an underground incinerator. He dug down at the side of the tank, made a hole in the side near the bottom and fitted a flexible flue liner to act as an airway to encourage combustion. He could now set fire to the contents at the bottom of the tank and, with the addition of a chimney, it worked perfectly. This lasted for ten years until the tank collapsed, so he went back to burying the carcasses.

Since April 2003, on-farm burial and burning in pits has been decreed illegal. There are no longer any knackers and the existence of hunts is threatened. It is an offence to leave a carcass unburied and a national pick-up service will probably cost £20 for removal and incineration. Manufacturers are offering small oil-fired incinerators that cost in the region of £8,000 each!

Dave experimented with a prototype wood-fuelled mobile incinerator that can be moved to where it is needed and well away from the village. It works well, is simple and convenient but incinerator rules then changed to requiring 'after burners', so making the sustainable one obsolete.

Chapter 58

"Eileen, could you find the 'phone number of either Wiltshire or Berkshire Police please?" Dave sounded worried; I had to ring him back as the police telephone numbers have all changed recently.

"What's the trouble?" I asked him when I rang with the information that he needed.

"I'll tell you about it when I come home."

When he arrived, he explained what had happened. He had gone to check on some sheep that are kept about ten miles away. He doesn't see them every day as the owner of the field looks at them to make sure they're all up the right way and soon lets Dave know if there's anything wrong.

When Dave approached the field where the sheep were kept, he climbed out of the Land Rover to open the gate, and could see the sheep which were three fields away, running about in an odd manner. Unfortunately he had several more gates to negotiate but he finally abandoned the Land Rover, grabbed his metal shepherd's crook, and started running.

He could see that there were two strange dogs with the sheep so intent on what they were doing that they were unaware of Dave's approach. One ewe lamb was held by the throat and being shaken around while the second dog was trying to savage another sheep. Dave used his crook in a way for which it was never intended; the dogs got the message and ran off, pursued by Dave shouting and waving his crook around. The dogs went through a hole in the hedge and by the time Dave found a gap to squeeze through, he heard a vehicle start up. Two men were in it and shouted to the dogs that jumped into the back. Dave was too far away to read the number plate and apart from the colour and possible make didn't have much description.

He returned to the flock of sheep which were beginning to settle down. One of the sheep had to be destroyed immediately (Dave always carries his humane killer in the Land Rover) and he brought the other one home for treatment.

The Police couldn't help but there had been problems with illegal hare coursing in the Thames Valley area. Dave suspected that the two men involved had been engaged in something similar.

Sheep are the most defenceless animals; they have nothing with which to defend themselves having no claws and only a few bottom teeth which are adapted to eating grass. The dogs were of the 'lurcher' type but any dog is a potential sheep worrier.

Dave once found a lurcher in with the sheep but could not manage to either catch it or chase it away. The bitch he had at that time was in season so he put her in his van and he enticed the stray dog into his van until he could find out whose it was. Jill was most upset at being yanked out of the van, she rather fancied the newcomer.

Chapter 59

Dave is gradually cutting back the sheep and reducing their numbers. He only has one flock on keep this year but is still retaining our 650 breeding ewes. He is due to retire in a couple of years and although has no intention of giving up sheep entirely, needs to have a more manageable system. There's plenty of land available in and around the village so the travelling will be less.

He has a lot of other commitments and is involved with Farm Crisis Network. This is an organization set up at the height of the B.S.E. crisis to help farmers, rather similar to the Samaritans. Farmers tend to be rather isolated and often need somebody to talk to about problems. There are so many forms to fill in now with penalties if they are filled in incorrectly and FCN people can support anxious farmers. There is a network of people connected with farming in various ways who man the telephone for at least four hours each week. They are able to put callers in touch with others who can answer their queries and know the relevant bodies to contact. This has also enabled him to speak at various functions arranged for the farming community around the country.

In the autumn of 2003 a day-long conference was organized for farmers in Devon under the auspices of Exeter Diocese. It was held at a Farm Theme Park near Buckfastleigh so during the breaks the park could be enjoyed. The conference itself was held in the theatre barn where usually various animals were shown. The seating consisted of wooden tiers upon which was placed carpet squares which were handed out on entry. There were four speakers including David but everyone was captivated when a lady spoke who had lost their whole beef herd to foot and mouth disease. Her daughter was expecting a baby but Denise was unable to leave the farm and we learnt at first hand just what grief was suffered by some people. Meals were laid on in the park restaurant and it was a great time to talk to each other and share experiences.

Chapter 60

Although there are less sheep there are still many problems to deal with. Although the winter is usually quieter, there is a lot of routine work to be done. The sheep require hay every day as the grass isn't growing and any wet weather turns the fields into quagmires under their feet. Some of the low-lying areas that are available to us may be partially under water which brings the problem of the mud snail! They are tiny, only 5-6 mm. long but in a square metre of habitat, there can be many hundreds. These pose a real hazard for sheep as they are the intermediary host for liver fluke, a rather nasty sheep disease. The eggs become attached to the herbage that is eaten by the sheep, and eventually grow into mature flukes that can produce a million eggs or more each during their lifetime. The animal loses condition progressively due to anaemia caused by the flukes living in the liver and bile ducts. Another symptom is 'bottle jaw' which shows as a swelling beneath the jaw caused by oedema. The eyes are watery and the membranes of the eye and other parts are very pale instead of a fresh pink colour. Sometimes in an apparently healthy sheep, death can occur suddenly and if a post mortem is performed it can be ascertained that an excessive number of flukes was the cause. If diagnosed in the flock, the other sheep can be treated with special medication and moved to higher ground with less possibility of the mud snail being present.

Dave has the seemingly never-ending task of chiropody! Sheep become lame very quickly, mainly due in the winter to mud between their toes which is easily dealt with. They can also suffer with 'foot rot', which is aggravated by wet conditions, so constant attention has to be paid and treatment given. Sometimes part of the hoof has to be cut away so that the infected part can be treated with anti-biotic spray. If the majority of the flock is affected, then the sheep have to stand in a footbath containing zinc sulphate for ten minutes. All these jobs are very smelly ones – either from the disease itself or the treatment that has to be given.

In the summer the problems are very different, especially amongst the ewes and lambs. Parasites, both internal and external, attack the vulnerable sheep.

The one that Dave dreads most is the blowfly. He calls it the 'battle of the blowfly' because it seems an endless war against them. This usually occurs when the weather is warm and humid when the lambs have stared eating lush, green grass and their bowels are a bit loose. If the lamb's tails haven't dropped off after rubber-ringing, the situation is bad as the wool round the tail becomes soiled. This provides an ideal place for the blowfly to lay its eggs – up to one hundred at a time. (The adult fly lays up to two or three thousand eggs in the month or so that it is alive.) The maggots hatch within a few hours and actually feed on the flesh of the sheep. This causes an intense itch and is extremely distressing to the sheep; she'll spend a lot of time trying to reach it with her mouth, which is often the first sign that there's anything wrong. If not noticed and treated, death can occur. Dave sprays around the tail and along the sheep's back with a chemical to try to prevent the blowflies.

Then there's the 'war on worms' – internal parasites that can cause stunted growth in the lambs. These intestinal worms are ingested as eggs that are present on the grass in fields where sheep with worms may have grazed some months before. As the ewes and lambs are moved to clean pastures after lambing, we manage to avoid this problem to a certain extent. These parasites can affect the lambs badly as the worms live inside their guts in large numbers (estimates of over 50,000 are not uncommon) and are less than 1cm. long and the thickness of a human hair. The lambs become dehydrated, they look unhappy and their ears droop – a sure sign that something is wrong! The treatment is prevention rather than cure and the sheep are routinely treated with anthelmintics. It is also a fact that one type of intestinal worm that lives in dogs can cause a disease called 'gid' in sheep. This has the same effect as a brain tumour and the sheep dies. It is important that people realise that dogs are wormed regularly, especially if they are exercised in fields where sheep graze.

Ticks also have to be tackled. They again are external parasites that live on a sheep's skin. They are not only an irritant to the sheep and lambs but can also cause disease in not only the sheep but in other animals too – even humans! If a tick is pulled off, it can leave its head behind attached to its host and will continue feeding on the victim's blood. There's a neat little gadget obtainable from the vet that can remove them easily – we had to use it on Kate recently. The treatment once again is preventative similar to that used for blowfly strike. The ewes used to be dipped every year but now it is permissible to use 'pour on' or 'jetting' procedures. It sometimes seems a miracle that sheep survive when there's so many seemingly innocent-looking, tiny organisms that can do so much damage.

Chapter 61

One day Dave had a bunch of fifty ewes but his business on that particular day was with their offspring which were with them, a total of about one hundred and fifty animals as most of the ewes had had twins. He set up the portable sheep race and the holding pen as he needed to vaccinate the lambs which, as you can imagine, is a very time consuming job. He decided to send Buddy to gather the sheep as there weren't too many and they soon started straggling across the field in the direction that the dog, guided by Dave's whistles was driving them. They were, as usual, very reluctant to enter the sheep pen; sheep always seem to be very suspicious animals. Dave had to help Buddy by shouting at the sheep (it sometimes works) and jumping up and down behind them. Eventually they were all in the pen but as he started to close the gate, one ewe took fright and darted back – accompanied by the two lambs.

Dave quickly put Bud back in the Land Rover and called Pip out. He managed to fetch the little family back to the pen where Dave tried to coax her in. He grabbed hold of one lamb but the ewe and the other lamb had made up their minds and ran off again.

Dave decided it was time for his 'Exocet' missile in the form of Woll and as the animals were at the other side of the field, he decided to take his motor bike. He worked the ewe across the field when suddenly she decided she'd had enough and did a 'belly flop'. Dave realized that if he was crafty, the lamb might return to its mother so he took his belt off and tied the ewe's legs together with it. She started bleating in protest but the lamb was completely confused and ran away. By this time, it had started raining and although Dave had a coat on, he was only wearing shorts and was tired and wet and the lamb had now gone through a gap in the hedge into a field of standing corn.

He was determined not to lose the lamb this time so went, on his motor bike, through the hedge too. The lamb, thankfully, had stayed in a 'tramline' so he was able to follow it quite easily but couldn't overtake it as the field sloped downwards and the lamb was travelling at speed. Eventually he caught it up when the lamb went through another hedge decided it couldn't run any more and flopped. Dave tipped the water out of his boots; they had got very wet as he rode through the corn. He picked up the lamb, turned the motor bike round, put the lamb on the petrol tank and reached round to grab the handlebars and set off back across the field. He went through the first hedge and was getting along nicely when the chain came off the motor bike!

As he couldn't put the lamb down while he replaced the chain, he dropped the motor bike and hoisted the lamb, which was a couple of months old and rather heavy, across his shoulders. He trudged back up the hill to the sheep pen where the forty-nine ewes were waiting patiently and gratefully lifted the lamb off his shoulders and into the pen. After he had finished the job that he had set out to do, he released the sheep, untied the recalcitrant ewe who soon found her lambs and let them feed.

This made Dave rather late coming home for his tea. Unfortunately, it was chips so he was greeted with,

"Where ever have you been?!"

Chapter 62

We are starting lambing this year in April with 70 older ewes still using an outdoor system but with access to a barn as well. Dave likes to keep the lambing fields just for the bulk of the flock. Last week he sold 120 in lamb Romneys at Ashford market. He's had them for three years and has had a good lambing percentage from the each year but felt that it was time to move them on while they still had a good value.

He's also assisting a neighbouring farmer with his rather haphazard lambing as he has no shepherd and the rams were left in with the ewes so they are having a rather protracted lambing season. Dave came home with a lamb about a month ago. The ewe had rejected it and although Dave had kept it going by holding it to other ewes to feed, it wasn't practical any more. It was a good strong lamb and took easily to feeding from a bottle. Soon it was able to live in the paddock behind the house with a nice shelter with lots of straw. Two little girls from along the lane started coming in after school to feed it, they called her 'Snowdrop'. When we went away for a weekend they fed the chickens and ducks for us too. Last Monday, however, I rushed out to fetch in the washing from the line as it had started raining, and realised, to my horror, that Snowdrop had died. I had the job of telling them as their Dad had already left to fetch them from school. They were very good about it and we decided that Snowdrop had had a good life – they still come in to feed the chickens though.

There is so much that can affect the lambs and it is an occupational hazard of trying to hand rear lambs. They are suicidal animals in any case. By far their favourite means of self destruction is strangling! If there is the shortest piece of baler twine looped in a pen a lamb will put its head into it and turn round until the twine tightens. Another means of death is by drowning and they are sometimes much older when they try this, they don't need much water either. David has to make sure that in a lamb water trough there is always a brick in it for them to stand on. A lamb managed somehow to get out of a pen, find its way across the yard to where there was a stopcock in the ground with water in the hole, fell into it, and drowned. Some very young lambs don't get out of the way when their Mum lies down and get squashed. They also run towards any moving vehicle enjoying running in front of large moving wheels.

The filling in of forms is one job that every farmer dreads. To claim subsidies that are lawfully due is a never ending task – especially when DEFRA change the criteria continuously. There was originally a scheme called 'variable premium,' which was worked by the difference in market price for the finished lamb and a European guaranteed price. This was then changed to 'headage payment' which was calculated by the number of ewes owned and for which one had 'quota'. Now there is another scheme, 'single farm payment' which is more complicated than ever and is based on acreage. As we own no land whatsoever, negotiations are under way with farmers whose land we utilize. There are seven books to be read and studied; if any details on the form are erroneous the claim is void. Our eldest grandson is sixteen and interested in agriculture but we wonder if there is going to be any future in it. David will be 65 in 2006 but would like to retain some sheep so that he can continue his interest and keep active. Unfortunately, he has arthritis in his hips and is finding it increasingly difficult to get around; the sheep can outrun him which is frustrating at lambing time. He utilizes a lot less land now and is able to rent quite a lot around the village so as the flock has decreased he's been able to concentrate his sheep enterprise closer to home.

We are still amazed at the variety of interesting occurrences that happen with the animals. Only this week a farmer, whose land Dave uses, and who has a few sheep of his own, sought Dave's help as a ewe was having difficulty giving birth to a large dead single lamb. Another ewe lambed shortly after, producing two healthy lambs. The second ewe, Charlotte, was the daughter of Katie, the other one. They've decided to share the raising of the twins who are as fat as butter, having two milk suppliers.

The hardest case this lambing, was this morning. He came in for some hot water as a ewe, having delivered a large lamb, had continued to strain and had pushed out her uterus. Having armed himself with a container of hot water, soap, disinfectant and a bowl he disappeared back to the lambing field, returning half an hour later for a well earned breakfast.

"Did you manage it?"

"Yes, but as I stood in the middle of the field with a string round my neck which was tied on to the ewe's back legs so that the appropriate part was accessible, I thought what a long way I had come since I performed a similar operation years ago in Kent!"

Sheep still have the same problems as do the shepherds but it is the job that David loved nearly fifty years ago. Inexplicable to anyone who has never had close contact with farm animals but Dave still cares as much for the latest weak, puny lamb as he did for the first one.

We've learnt so much about life from the sheep and can see many parallels in our lives and can look forward to the future knowing that it is in the hands of the Good Shepherd who cares for His sheep.

~ End ~